Healing
the
Wounded
Soul

Healing
the
Wounded
Soul

by

Phyllis K. Peterson

Bahá'í
PUBLISHING
Wilmette, Illinois

Bahá'í Publishing, 415 Linden Avenue, Wilmette, IL 60091-2844

08 07 06 05   4 3 2 1

Library of Congress Cataloging-in-Publication Data
Peterson, Phyllis, 1941–
        Healing the wounded soul / by Phyllis K. Peterson.
            p. cm.
        Includes bibliographical references.
        ISBN 1-931847-25-8 (alk. Paper)
            1. Peterson, Phyllis, 1941– 2. Bahais—United States—
Biography. 3. Adult child sexual abuse victims—United States—
Biography. 4. Family violence—religious aspects—Bahai Faith. I.
Title.

BP395.P48A3 2005
297.9'3'092—dc22
[B]
                                                        2005048280

Cover design by Robert A. Reddy
Book design by Suni D. Hannan

Contents

Foreword

Healing the Wounded Soul should be required reading for anyone wishing to understand the impact of childhood sexual abuse on children and families. Phyllis Peterson's powerful descriptions of her abusive experiences during her childhood, coupled with her lucid and compelling descriptions of the impact these early experiences had on her later life, are sure to educate everyone about the horrors of childhood sexual abuse and its long-lasting negative effects upon individuals and families.

As a clinical psychologist who has worked for over twenty years with adult survivors of sexual abuse, I applaud Ms. Peterson's willingness to be completely honest and forthright about even the most painful and humiliating life experiences. Her descriptions ring true. She offers these details not as a lament to her suffering but as a tribute to the amazing power of the human spirit to triumph over even the most daunting challenges. Unaided by parents, unable to turn to friends or family members for guidance or assistance, she set out alone upon a quest for truth that led her to the world's spiritual traditions. Drawn to elements of all of them, she ultimately chose the Bahá'í Faith as her guide. She was drawn to its inclusiveness and its message of equality for all human beings. She was also attracted to its practicality and the applicability of its writings and scriptures to her own plight.

Through a series of stormy ups and downs, Ms. Peterson's quest to heal and reform her own overly sexualized identity according to the spiritual guidelines she found in Bahá'í texts led her to a point of health and happiness. She discusses many of the guidelines that were helpful to her and includes direct quotes from Bahá'í scripture to support her discussion. These guidelines included the advice to seek the help of competent physicians when one is mentally or physically ill. Ms. Peterson heeded this advice, but while psychotherapy and medication were an important part of her healing journey, they were not the bedrock. For her, the foundation of her remarkable transformation was the healing power of God.

The strengths of Ms. Peterson's book are many, but I am particularly struck with her chapters about breaking the intergenerational cycle of abuse and the appendix on chastity. Her ability to take responsibility for mistreatment of her daughter while remaining compassionate toward herself is a model for all to follow. She clearly shows how the cycle of abuse ensnares generation after generation. In a touching letter to her daughter, she takes responsibility for past mistakes while avoiding the pitfall of self-condemnation. She sings praises for her own strength and courage in the face of almost overwhelming obstacles even as she owns up to the damage done to her daughter while her healing process was in its infancy.

In her thought provoking chapter on chastity, Ms. Peterson reviews the Bahá'í position on the purpose and meaning of the sexual instinct and compares it with today's cultural standards. She argues that sexuality as it manifests in a person's life is not purely instinctual but is an interplay of biology, learning, and personal choice. She points out that childhood traumas can heavily influence adult sexuality and that unhealed wounds can impair the formation of truly intimate bonds later in life. She does an excellent job of contrasting emotional intimacy with what she calls "genital" intimacy and makes the case that promiscuous sex leaves one hungry for true emotional closeness.

Her advice to parents who are concerned about protecting their children from abusive experiences echoes the best scientific advice of the day. She attempts to dispel some of the myths that surround sexual abuse and gives advice about dealing with the issue in a straightforward, open fashion. She warns parents that vigilance is warranted in our highly sexualized culture.

In addition to my work as a clinical psychologist, I also work in forensic psychology, the discipline that addresses the overlap of psychology and the law. In this capacity I have become acquainted with the impact of institutions on the perpetuation of childhood sex abuse. Organizations that lack clear policies and procedures to protect children can unwittingly become a safe haven for child abusers who pose under the guise of "helpers" or "teachers" of children. Appendix 2 includes an official policy statement of the national governing body of the Bahá'í Faith in the United States about protecting children from sexual abuse. I am very pleased to see that this organization has taken this step. The alarming proliferation of childhood sexual abuse and the scandals that have touched even the most historically sacred of institutions such as the Roman Catholic Church show us that organizational vigilance and an active approach to protecting children are absolutely necessary.

Gone are the days when any one of us can responsibly take the position that the sexual abuse of children happens somewhere else to someone else. These things can and do happen every day in all of our neighborhoods, schools, and organizations. It is up to everyone to do all that we can to stop these cycles of abuse before they start and to help bring healing to those who have survived these experiences.

I applaud Ms. Peterson's courageous willingness to give her all in this endeavor. I highly recommend this book to everyone, but especially to parents, teachers, counselors, health professionals, and all those who work with children.

—Patricia Romano McGraw, Ph.D.
Author of *It's Not Your Fault: How Healing Relationships Change Your Brain & Can Help You Overcome a Painful Past*

Acknowledgments

Patricia Romano McGraw worked as a coauthor of this book, offering her professional insights into my experiences. Her therapeutic explanations of what I was going through in the early years of my recovery were enlightening and validating. As a consequence I have gained even more healing knowledge about myself and the Bahá'í revelation. Any wounded soul can benefit from reading this point and counterpoint offering of staggering suffering and shame with her supportive, professional understanding. It can ground one from any religious background, for it truly unites science with religion.

I also want to honor my editor, Terry Cassiday, whose hand has blessed every page and who has been the strongest supporter of my voice, offering encouragement every step of the way. I am grateful to her beyond words. Terry, Patricia, Christopher Martin, and Bahhaj Taherzadeh reconstructed my manuscript and turned it into a valuable tool for the healing of the wounded soul.

My family has believed in me through all my ups and downs, and I want to acknowledge the fact that they continue to be healthy and strong and strive toward unity. Thank you one and all!

Introduction

The best beloved of all things in My sight is Justice; turn not away therefrom if thou desirest Me, and neglect it not that I may confide in thee. By its aid thou shalt see with thine own eyes and not through the eyes of others, and shalt know of thine own knowledge and not through the knowledge of thy neighbor. Ponder this in thy heart, how it behooveth thee to be. Verily justice is My gift to thee and the sign of My loving-kindness. Set it then before thine eyes.

—*Bahá'u'lláh*

I write this book as your sister and your friend. I write it with the desire to share with you what I have learned about healing from childhood sexual abuse. I do not claim to be unique. Quite the contrary. I offer my story to you, the reader, so that you will not feel alone if you, too, are dealing with all the many issues that surround childhood sexual abuse.

If you are an adult survivor yourself, I hope you will find my story encouraging. Although it has taken me a long time to heal, I now enjoy a spiritual happiness and peace of mind that I know is the fruit of my long struggle to overcome the spiritual, emotional, and behavioral obstacles that separated me from my true identity, my spiritual identity. I want to assure you that this is possible for you, too.

If you are currently in the grip of an abusive relationship, I hope you will find guidance in these pages that will encourage you to escape the oppression and tyranny from which you suffer. I hope you will find spiritual empowerment in the Bahá'í writings, which so clearly state that fair and just treatment for all is the way of life ordained by God. Clearly the Bahá'í Faith, with its emphasis on unity and justice, is your ally in your fight to escape tyranny, oppression, and control by those who would do you harm.

If you are a young person who is being hurt by someone older than you, someone in authority over you, I hope you will find information here that will tell you what to do to get out of this situation. It is not good for you to remain in this type of situation. It is important for you to understand that whether an abusive person realizes it at the time or not, your efforts to end the abuse are the best thing you can do both for yourself and for the abuser. Abusive persons, as you will read in these pages, are often acting out their own unresolved pain. They cannot begin to heal as long as the acting out behavior takes the place of self-examination and taking responsibility for one's own life.

If you yourself are abusing someone, please read this book and begin to reflect on the terrible long-term consequences of your actions. Not only are you hurting the person you are abusing, you are harming yourself spiritually and setting up ripples of pain that can extend through generations. You are a person who needs education and forgiveness. But none of the good things that await you can be yours until you take responsibility for your life and begin your own healing journey. The Bahá'í Faith stands ready to guide, forgive, and help you stay on your own spiritual pathway.

If you feel that this issue does not touch you and that you have no need to read this book, I encourage you to read it anyway, for you are in denial. Oppression is worldwide, and children, who are the least powerful and most vulnerable among us, often become the victims of those who seek to exploit. Specifically, childhood sexual abuse is spreading in epidemic proportions. The understanding and help of everyone is needed if we are to end this terrible blight.

It is important for each of us to realize that the search for the end of abuse of power is not just a personal journey. A document issued by the Bahá'í International Community titled *The Prosperity of Humankind* states, "Justice is the one power that can translate the dawning consciousness of humanity's oneness into a collective will." The statement names justice as the key to the ultimate peace and unity of planet earth:

> At the individual level, justice is that faculty of the human soul that enables each person to distinguish truth from falsehood. In the sight of God, Bahá'u'lláh avers, justice is "the best beloved of all things" since it permits each individual to see with his own eyes rather than the eyes of others, to know through his own knowledge rather than the knowledge of his neighbor or his group. It calls for fair-mindedness in one's judgments, for equity in one's treatment of others, and is thus a constant if demanding companion in the daily occasions of life.[1]

My personal story, which you will read in the following pages, is the story of my search for truth and justice. My journey led me in many directions. It was not a smooth, easy, or unidirectional process. At times it was very chaotic. I myself not only was a victim of abuse, I became abusive to those I love most dearly. Many times I thought all was lost. Many times I thought it might be better for my life to end rather than continue on its erratic, chaotic, and sometimes destructive path.

For me, distrust of authority, all authority, formed a major roadblock to my healing. I rejected all forms of control over me, including religious teachings. I felt that all too often "religion" had been used as an excuse for opportunists to manipulate, oppress, and control people for their own ends. You will read in these pages that my rebellious state of mind left me floundering with nothing but my own distorted view of the world. How could I know how to live when my early childhood experiences were so full of pain, confusion, and more pain? Where was I to find a prescription for living that I could trust?

In 1969 I discovered the Bahá'í Faith and its scriptures. I was immediately impressed with the religion's emphasis on justice. "The light of men is Justice," its Prophet and Founder, Bahá'u'lláh, says. "Quench it not with the contrary winds of oppression and tyranny. The purpose of justice is the appearance of unity among men. The ocean of divine wisdom surgeth within this exalted word, while the books of the world cannot contain its inner significance."[2] Words such as these began to help me realize I could use the wisdom of the Bahá'í Faith and other religious wisdom as a guidebook for living.

I also began to understand that my struggle was part of a larger spiritual process that the world was now undergoing. This process will ultimately bring about the peace and harmony of all the peoples of the earth. Each and every human soul is a part of that process. That means me, and that means you, too. *The Prosperity of Humankind* also states, "The activity most intimately linked to the consciousness that distinguishes human nature is the individual's exploration of reality for himself or herself. The freedom to investigate the purpose of existence and to develop the endowments of human nature that make it achievable requires protection. Human beings must be free to know."[3]

In a nutshell, this statement about the exploration of reality sums up my process. I grew up oppressed and unprotected. I was not free. I did not know about justice, and, most frightening of all, I did not know myself. I could not feel my own feelings. I could not think clear and rational thoughts. I behaved in ways that I found reprehensible. I was not me. These pages trace the progress of my discovery of myself. At the core of me I found my link with God and with all mankind. I hope you will find something in these pages that will inspire you in your own journey to find your spiritual identity, an identity that links you with me, with others, and with God.

Chapter 1, "My Own Story," is the beginning of my personal story. In it I discuss my "family inheritance," which was abuse. I talk about keeping the abuse a secret and about the emotional roller coaster that ensued. I speak about my problems with authority and about the sexual acting out that took over my life. My first encounter with the Bahá'í Faith was seminal. That is where I first encountered the idea of justice and the concept of making a personal search for truth. However, the things I was learning did not take root immediately. The process as it unfolded is described in chapter 2.

In chapter 2, "Searching for Spiritual Identity," I discuss my dawning awareness of my true spiritual identity and the gradual discovery of my own spiritual powers: the power of understanding, thought and reasoning, reflection, discernment, and others. I began to realize that it was my job to investigate reality and make up my own mind about what truth and justice meant for me and my life. The central realization was that I could choose how to live and who to be. I could be a tyrant and a monster, or a saint, as it were. The choice was up to me. These new realizations did not come easily. I passed through periods of severe mental illness that included debilitating paranoia and the irrational thinking of psychosis. It was not until I endured a longer period of instability that I finally became clear about the need to not only think and feel differently, but also to act differently, to conform my behavior to a code of conduct. This is the part of my life I discuss in chapter 3.

In chapter 3, "Turning to the Light," I discuss the dual nature of humanity that includes the potential to be as heavenly as the angels or more debased than the beasts of the fields. I came to understand my own free will as a pivot point that propelled me in one direction or the other. Pulled, it seemed, by almost irresistible forces rooted in my childhood of abuse, I found I had to exert maximum effort to keep myself on my chosen path of virtuous behavior. The struggle was exhausting, and at times I wondered if I should just give up. It helped me to realize that everyone, abused or not, goes through many of the same spiritual struggles. All human beings have this dual nature, and everyone must make choices that accumulate to determine their character and identity.

In chapter 4, "Telling the Secret," I explain that it was not until I finally had the courage to end the silence about my history of childhood sexual abuse that a definitive change took place in my life. Once I did, the sexual passions and temptations that had dogged me were finally linked clearly in my own mind to my history of childhood sexual abuse. I could see that expressing my pain and rage about my past enabled me to access my emotions in the present. I found I had so many new things to learn. I learned about boundaries and saying "no." I learned how to speak about my own experiences honestly and how to express my emotions truthfully. And, most importantly, I learned the value of obedience. The Bahá'í scriptures to which I was turning increasingly for guidance enjoin those with mental health issues to seek in times of sickness the help of "competent physicians."[4] I took that advice and found that psychotherapy and medication helped stabilize my emotions, allowing me further control and stability in my life.

Chapter 5, "Breaking the Intergenerational Cycle of Abuse," is most precious to me. My oldest daughter had been with me during the darkest days of my illness and immersion in the nightmarish acting out of my own history of abuse. As I became healthy, I was filled with the agony of realizing that my daughter had scars—many scars—because of the way I had treated her when she was a child. In this chapter I share a letter that I wrote to her to acknowledge her pain. Without acknowledgment, decades of pain will ache untended, and decades of fragmented memories will remain unresolved. Such pain creates immobilizing mental, emotional, and physical distress and results in the unconscious perpetration of abuse down through the generations. The letter to my daughter acknowledges my role in her life, but it also encourages her to take an active role in ending the cycle of abuse. In it I make suggestions to her, encouraging her now in positive directions. Now that I am healthier, I can see these directions and give this advice, an ability I did not have when my daughter was small.

In chapter 6, "The Spiritual Aspects of Suffering," I briefly discuss the mystery of suffering and its quickening effect on the soul. It is a paradoxical fact that the greatest and most holy of men and women seem to have suffered the most. I share here selections from Bahá'í texts that have brought much comfort to me in my healing journey. Among the selections are passages that explain the hidden benefits of suffering, the meaning of suffering, accepting life's difficulties, and a collection of beautiful and powerful prayers from Bahá'í scripture for assistance and protection.

In chapter 7, "Preventing and Treating Child Sexual Abuse," I present some of the conventional wisdom on the subject. The statistics on child sex abuse are staggering. There is literally an epidemic of child abuse running rampant in all parts of the globe. It is everyone's job to try to end this abuse and protect our children. The fate of the future of the planet depends on the success of our efforts.

Appendix 1 presents a document written by the international governing body of the Bahá'í Faith on the subject of domestic violence, which includes the sexual abuse of children. Appendix 2 presents a policy statement of the national governing body of the Bahá'í

Faith in the United States on the subject. I include these materials because they indicate the strong position that the Bahá'í Faith takes against childhood sexual abuse and the actions that the institutions of the Faith are taking to prevent it.

Appendix 3 is about teaching protective behaviors to young children. It can help parents and teachers educate children about how to set boundaries with others who might harm them. It can also help parents and teachers prepare children so they will know what to say and do to avoid becoming a victim.

Appendix 4 is a letter about the spiritual law of chastity revealed by Bahá'u'lláh, the Prophet and Founder of the Bahá'í Faith. I wrote the letter both to educate myself and in an effort to assist friends who are struggling to live according to the high moral standard of chastity.

It is my dearest hope that something in the pages that follow will be of assistance to you, whatever your situation may be, so that you, too, may find greater happiness and play a role in helping to end childhood sexual abuse.

1

My Own Story

For many years I had a recurring nightmare. I would dream that someone was approaching my bed in the dark. Try as I might, I could not escape my bed. I was paralyzed, powerless. I would try to open my mouth to scream, but it, too, was paralyzed. A level of consciousness would penetrate my nightmare, and I could actually hear myself emitting nonverbal, guttural sounds even though my lips were sealed tightly. Yet I couldn't wake myself sufficiently during the dream to end this terror. I would awaken later, drenched with sweat, exhausted, and fearful of going back to sleep.

🐜 🐜 🐜

At the age of two I liked to be held. Like any normal, healthy child, I enjoyed being touched. I was too young to know the difference between a loving touch and a secret touch. There was no one to protect my innocence, no one to keep me safe until I was old enough to protect myself. No one witnessed the sexual abuse my father practiced on me when I was a little girl. No one in my family recognized the need for physical, spatial, or sexual boundaries in one so young.

Most of the abuse I experienced happened when I was in bed, sleeping. My father would come to my room at night, when my mother was asleep and it was safe for him. As the years passed and I grew older, I became more wakeful during these episodes, yet I knew instinctively that I was not supposed to be aware of what he was doing to me with his hands.

There was no one to protect me from the abuse, and I was too young to recognize wrong or to gainsay my father, who, as patriarch of an old-fashioned German-Italian family, demanded complete obedience to his authority. I did not know then, of course, that I would seek for the rest of my life to repair the damage that my father was doing. This sexual abuse continued for six years.

One day when I was eight years old, I was chatting and playing in the living room, one of six happy children, when my father entered the room and sat down in an easy chair. He called me to him. Passively and obediently I went to him. He pulled me up onto his lap and placed his hand under my dress, inside my panties. My mother was in the kitchen, unaware. I sat on his lap while yet again he abused me sexually. I cannot remember feeling any shame; how sad and strange it seems to me now.

Then one day I believe the hand of God intervened. My oldest sister told my mother what was happening. My mother lay awake that night, pretending to be asleep. When my father got out of bed and stealthily approached my bedroom, she sat up and asked him what he was doing. He told her he was checking on the children. She confronted him with my sister's accusation. He admitted his wrongdoing. My mother told him that from then on she would be responsible for checking on the children.

Abuse: A Family Inheritance

As I later learned, my father had been severely abused as a child by my grandfather physically, if not sexually. My grandfather was an alcoholic and may even have been psychotic at times. He seemed to hate my father as evidenced in the fact that he beat him regularly and treated him as a slave to the rest of the family. Though all of my father's siblings were abused, my father was abused more than the others.

My grandfather is known to have committed bestiality, and I believe he may have perpetrated a very aggressive type of sexual abuse on his children. My father's sister has told me that when my father was about ten years old, she saw him run out of the barn completely naked, crying so hard that his eyes were swollen shut. I have also been told that when he was fifteen years old, the police locked him up in the local jail to protect him from my grandfather, who was chasing him with an ax. I am also told that my grandfather beat my father regularly with a bullwhip.

My father was artistic, but he hid this side of himself and destroyed his sketches because he feared the ridicule and abuse of others. In his family, daring to express his thoughts and dreams brought punishment and judgment because it was their habit to ridicule and belittle one another cruelly. There was no chance for his artistic talent, or even for his mental faculties, to develop fully; he had been forced to quit school in the eighth grade to work and help support the family. For the rest of his life, he was frustrated by his inability to read well enough even to understand newspaper articles.

Following in my grandfather's footsteps, my father ran his home in an extremely authoritarian manner, requiring complete obedience from his children. Like his father, he was brutally abusive to his children. He would not allow any of us to speak without intimidating or ridiculing us; we children were not allowed to speak while eating, working, or preparing for bed. We had to whisper to each other, and if we were heard whispering in bed, we were berated or beaten.

My father had a perverse sense of humor and seemed to be obsessed with sex. When my sisters and I were in our teens, he falsely accused us of "whoring around." The truth was, we were extremely unsophisticated children who were sheltered socially by his fears. I am assuming that his guilty conscience and his own obsession with sex drove him to forbid our participation in extracurricular activities at school so that he could keep a watchful eye on us.

The only respite we had from our father was when he was at work, when we were sent to the movies once a week on Saturday, or when we attended school or church. I learned never to stay at home when I could escape to church, and I never invited anyone to my home. Even today I find myself feeling sad and anxious if I stay in my house for too many hours in one day.

Keeping the Secret

Though today I have told my story many times over, the majority of my childhood was governed by "the secret." In 1986, at the age of forty-six, I wrote in my journal the following entry, which probably could have been written by virtually any survivor of childhood sexual abuse:

Please don't look too closely at me. You might see my secret. Please don't talk to me. I might accidentally tell you my secret. No, I don't want to be friends. Friends tell secrets. No, I don't want that promotion. I'm too occupied with my secret. And I can't express an opinion either. You might guess my secret. No, I'm not going to invite you to my home. We have a houseful of secrets! What's the sense of sharing feelings? People with secrets avoid them. And no, I can't tell you what my secret is. It's so secret, I may not be fully conscious of it.

This is the universal power of the secret. To protect their secrets, survivors of childhood sexual abuse withdraw into themselves, always keeping others at a distance. I had decided to protect my family at all costs, to be "perfect," and never to talk to anyone about my abuse. I had decided to avoid asking questions, to be obedient at all times, to be passive and compliant, and never to express anger about anything. I was afraid that if I were to do otherwise, people would think I was crazy and would lock me up or beat me. I guess you could say I had chosen to completely suppress my identity.

"Behave, or we'll lock you in the basement!" "Be good, or we'll put you in reform school!" "Be loyal to the family at all costs, or all of your brothers and sisters will be put in the children's home or foster homes!" These threats echoed in my mind. What kind of fear and desperation must have driven my parents to give their children such messages! That is the power of the secret. My parents kept the secret. Aunts and uncles kept the secret. Grandparents kept the secret. We children kept the secret.

An Emotional Roller Coaster

A number of factors made me feel I was to blame for what had happened to me. The silence surrounding the issue and the fact that I was my father's "favorite child" made me think the abuse was somehow my fault. During my teenage years I attended a Baptist church in Rockford, Illinois. There I learned about the Christian doctrine of original sin while watching a film depicting people screaming and burning in hell. This, to me, at the tender age of ten in 1951, confirmed that I was to blame for what had happened to me. I knew then that I had participated in something evil, yet I also realized that my father—at that time the most important authority figure in my life—had implicitly condoned it. Thus began a conflict of values that I was to act out in self-destructive ways for the next forty-five years. This moral conflict tormented me emotionally, even though I could not identify or articulate it.

The sexual abuse I had experienced as a very young child had shaped my identity and awakened in me feelings and impulses that would not go away. I could neither understand nor describe them, but I knew they were inappropriate. I learned to avoid dealing with these feelings and impulses at all costs. Yet, during my teenage years, when my peers were dealing with the normal physical and emotional changes that accompany puberty, I began to have the terrifying feeling that I was sliding out of control. There was no one to help me make sense of the emotional roller coaster I was experiencing. I was not promiscuous, but my buried thoughts and sexual fantasies were becoming more and more threatening. I had the strange feeling of wanting to do things I knew were wrong and at the same time wanting to resist these impulses. I felt the urge to act on these fantasies, but the thought of doing so was abhorrent to me. Because I was unable to understand or explain the conflict that was going on inside me, I would find myself doing things and then later I would have the feeling it wasn't really me doing them. I found myself behaving seductively in ways that were sometimes subtle and sometimes blatant. I felt tormented.

When I was fourteen years old, I was attracted to a married man in our neighborhood. I pretended to visit his wife, then I teased him seductively, not fully understanding the effect of my actions until one day he violently pushed me against the wall and pressed his full body against mine. I felt great shame. I didn't think that was what I wanted. Was my behavior just the result of a teenager's raging hormones—my coming of age as a woman, so to speak? I don't think so.

What was the real reason I visited the Army, Navy, and Air Force enlistment offices regularly on a weekly basis from the age of fifteen to seventeen? I believe that raging hormones teamed with parental authority that had covertly condoned sexual activity by encouraging sexual feelings in me as a small child had made sex the unconscious and unintentional focus of my life.

One day I sat on a youth's lap in church. On another occasion I sat on a young man's lap in my home economics class. When the teacher came into the classroom and found me that way, she scolded me and sent me to the office. Clearly this was inappropriate behavior, but in retrospect it is certainly understandable that someone who had been sexually abused on her father's lap might behave this way. But no one—not even I—made the connection at the time. It never occurred to me that I was acting out sexually to vent painful emotions from the past. It was as if I had unconscious sexual power that was approved by my father yet forbidden. I was drawn to anything with even a vapor of seduction, such as the suggestive lifting of an eyebrow on a movie star's face, and instantly I would add it to my collection of subtle seductive tricks.

As a result of such incidents, I became morally hypervigilant as a young adult. I thought I needed to protect myself from some external threat. Little did I know that the real threat was the sexual side of me—the side I was trying so hard to suppress—which was becoming more and more active. The excessive sexual content of my thoughts was becoming increasingly frightening to me.

I was making a conscious effort to live what I perceived to be a good, moral life, but my behavior was contradicting that morality and seemed beyond my control. There were times when I would become aware of my own inappropriate behavior. I was dumbfounded by it and felt ashamed of the moral inconsistencies between what I believed and what I did and would punish myself for the transgressions I felt I had committed. I would redouble my efforts at self-control and vigilantly guard against external threats or temptations, yet eventually I would lapse again into unconscious behavior that betrayed what I was trying so desperately to hide.

In August of 1959, my church awarded me with a music scholarship to attend the Baptist Bible College in Denver, Colorado. This is where I met my first husband on a blind date on January 8, 1960. We saw each other every day for two weeks. I violated the school's rules by going to the theater to see the movie *Porgy and Bess*. At the end of January, the dean of the school sent me home in shame because I was suspected to be sleeping with the young man I was dating. It didn't matter that the accusations weren't true; I was forced to leave. The young man asked me to marry him before I left Denver. I said "yes," and it was decided that I would return home and wait until he sent for me. He was in the Air Force, and I went home to work for a finance company for a month, earning enough money to take the bus to Kansas City, Missouri, where my fiancé's mother lived at the time.

My father was angry when he heard the news. "If you run away to marry him, I'll follow you, and I'll find you. I'll tell him you have nigger blood in you so he won't want to marry you. So no one will want to marry you, you whore!" he said. With my mother's assistance I called the police. They escorted me to the bus station, where my mother met me to say goodbye. I left Rockford frightened and dejected.

I had left college in shame because there had been no one to act as my advocate; I had left home in shame with the label "whore" ringing in my ears; and I was now leaving my innocent, defenseless brothers and sisters in an extremely violent home environment with no hope of safety, love, or protection from our raging father. As I sat behind the bus driver, my shame increased as I allowed him to run his hand up and down my leg in the dark. I wondered how I could allow that when I claimed to love the man I was going to meet in Kansas City, yet I could not bring myself to stop what I knew was inappropriate behavior. I took a taxi to my future mother-in-law's home, aware that I was in danger of acting out sexually with the taxi driver. I stayed in Kansas City until my future husband had transferred to Texas. His mother bought me a wedding dress before I left to join him in Fort Worth in March 1960.

I was terrified that my father had somehow followed me to Texas. After I arrived I found myself constantly looking over my shoulder, watching for his green pickup truck. Every time I saw a green truck, I felt a rush of adrenalin and picked up my pace to duck inside a store. I was that terrified.

My husband and I were married on April 16, 1960. I became pregnant the following month. I was nauseated for a full five-and-a-half months and lost twenty pounds. It is not surprising that my daughter was such a tiny baby when she was born. I was so sick, it's a wonder she got any nourishment at all.

A complicating factor was that my husband and I didn't have enough money for food during my pregnancy. My husband was an Airman Third Class in the Air Force, and his salary barely provided enough money for us to eat anything more than soup—certainly no meat. I believe my baby's development in the womb was saved by the fact that I was taking prenatal vitamins. I was starving and nauseated at the same time. My husband didn't understand that I wasn't getting enough to eat, and I didn't know how to tell him. I couldn't ask him for money because I didn't know how. It was my perception that I wasn't allowed to ask for money—not from my parents, not from my husband.

I slept through much of my pregnancy. My husband didn't know what behavior to expect of a pregnant woman, nor did he know what my needs might be, but he really did his best to care for us, given the little knowledge he had. He also didn't recognize that the inordinate amount of time I spent sleeping was not merely a result of the changes in my body that were caused by the pregnancy, but a symptom of deep depression and a desire to escape.

My daughter was born at Carswell Air Force Base Hospital in Fort Worth, Texas, on February 8, 1961. I was nineteen years old. I recall being sad and very disturbed because my mother couldn't come to visit while I was in the hospital. I remember crying. The nurses said that I was too emotionally upset for my milk to "come down." I tried again and again to nurse my baby, but apparently she wasn't getting any nourishment. In fact, she was losing weight. She had weighed 5 pounds, 4 ounces at birth and went down to 4 pounds, 10 ounces after three days. At that point the nurses took matters into their own hands and began giving my baby a bottle. The hospital policy stated that babies who weighed less than 5 pounds could not leave the hospital until they reached 5 pounds. I was sent home, but they kept my baby for seven days before allowing me to take her home. I was utterly distraught.

When my baby finally did come home, she was not very responsive. It seemed as though she did not smile throughout her infancy. I was inept. My husband had to prepare the baby's formula for me. I didn't know how to do it and couldn't seem to summon the energy or the will to figure it out, but my husband could. At that time in my life, I just let people move me around, and things just happened. I didn't make them happen. Things worked because everyone told me what to do. My husband always knew what to do, and I trusted that. Life was very simple for me because I didn't make any choices.

I remember being proud of my baby and wanting to be a good mother, but I felt as if I needed to have someone there with me. I needed someone to watch me so I would be good, so I would do the right things the right way. It was as though I couldn't be good—couldn't behave appropriately—unless there were someone there to be good in front of. This thought was continually part of my consciousness. I didn't know how to act; it was as if I were not fully conscious.

One of the things that helped me to become more conscious was the positive attention I received from my husband's grandparents, our daughter's great-grandparents—Grandma and Grandpa Stone. We brought our baby to visit their farm in Durant, Oklahoma, and received many gifts from them.

Some months later we returned to Durant, and Grandma Stone commented on the baby's lack of weight gain. At this point I was beginning to feel even more inept. The fact that I had left my sisters and brothers in danger was ever present in my mind. I was preoccupied with this thought. I couldn't always remember to feed my baby and take care of her needs. She developed a diaper rash, of which I was very ashamed. It developed into large, open, painful sores all over her bottom. I tried everything I could think of to treat the rash—powders, lotions, creams. However, I left my daughter in her wet diapers far too long, for hours sometimes. I just couldn't remember to change her diapers as often as they needed to be changed. I was spending a great deal of time sleeping. The smell of ammonia from my daughter's diapers was fierce and overpowering, and the sores clearly must have been very painful, but she was stoic and did not cry about them. She tried to move away from the diaper to keep it from touching the sores, but she did not cry. Grandma Stone must have been very shocked. The open sores finally healed when my daughter was potty trained, but there were scars on her bottom. I was so ashamed. I had no one with whom to share my shame, my thoughts, or my worries.

I also couldn't remember to feed my daughter regularly. I wanted to sleep, and she would cry. I would get up and feed her a cracker to quiet her, then I would go back to bed. This, of course, was not sufficient. I think I couldn't remember to feed her because no one was present to watch. Then, one day, I believe God intervened. I picked up a magazine and began reading a story about a woman who was an alcoholic. She was so drunk that when her baby in the playpen cried, she threw her a cracker to quiet her. If the mother was drunk all day, the baby ate nothing but crackers all day. It was a sobering story for me, and I began to try harder.

In my shame and out of eagerness to correct my ways, I tried suddenly to introduce new foods to my baby. Unfortunately, she gagged on the new foods. I didn't know that new foods should be introduced to a baby gradually and in small amounts. I was discouraged. I felt as if my baby were fighting me. This was the beginning of my efforts to dominate her. I felt I had to coerce my daughter to eat her food, to take medicine, to accept ear drops. I equated forcing her to do what I thought was right with being the best mother I could be.

It's not surprising that I became an authoritarian parent, given my authoritarian upbringing and my mindset at the time. My mindset had been formed not only by a punitive upbringing but also by my fear of a punitive God and the concept of original sin. This indoctrination dogged my heels in every church I attended and shaped my relationship with my children.

Twenty-two months separated the birth of my first child from that of my second, also a girl. This time I had more experience with motherhood, and I felt more confident. I was less rigid in my attitude toward this child, though my habitual inflexibility persisted with my older daughter. In 1963 I gave birth to a son, to whom I showed great favor because he was the only male child.

Unfortunately, my husband and my children all suffered from the fact that we did not know how the sexual abuse perpetrated against me during childhood had affected our family. I never revealed my secret to my husband. I thought that no man would want me as his wife if he were to know the truth. I was never unfaithful to him in the sense that violation of marriage vows would imply, but I could never reconcile my unfaithful thoughts and impulses. I believed I was damned because of my secret character. I was convinced that it was rooted in the Christian doctrine of original sin.

Authority, Power, Oppression

My childhood experiences had left me feeling very, very confused about the whole issue of authority. The dictionary defines authority as "the power to influence or command thought, opinion, or behavior."[1] It also defines it as the source from which power emanates and associates it with the person who commands this power. I had almost no experience and no understanding of what it meant to use power justly. I had experienced so much oppression in the form of abuse from my father that I had no idea how to center my life—how to find a focus, a meaning, and most importantly how to find a source of guidance and direction that would enable me to take control of my own life.

The dictionary defines oppression as "unjust or cruel exercise of authority or power," and it goes on to give another definition, "a sense of being weighed down in body or mind."[2] That was an apt description for how I felt—I was weighed down—so weighed down and so confused that I swung madly from one extreme to another. I wanted very much to take control of my life and my own behavior, but so often when I would try to implement my independence, I would crumble and collapse at the slightest criticism or resistance. I was so anxious to please and so uncertain of myself that I was bound to fail in my efforts. I became literally paranoid.

Reeling Out of Control

For me, the central and most debilitating aspect of my own childhood sexual abuse was that it not only made me fearful of exercis-
ing authority over others and fearful of being harshly judged by
those in authority over me, it literally robbed me of my own sense
of power and authority over myself. My experiences left me feeling
powerless—weak, ineffectual, floundering in life. Ongoing crises
in my life kept me reeling from one disastrous situation to another.
I experienced a self-hatred that played itself out in risky, self-de-
feating, and self-destructive behavior. When people would try to
get close to help me, I would rebel and push them away. No one
was ever going to have power over me again, I would tell myself.

First Glimmer

For me, the first glimmer of a way out of this trap occurred when
my husband and I were transferred from Fort Worth to Okinawa,
Japan. Two major things happened to me in Okinawa. First, I was
exposed to a multitude of religious beliefs that led me to question
Christianity as it had been taught to me. My husband and I attended services at the base chapel, which held rotating services for
all. Lutherans, Presbyterians, Catholics, Methodists, and members
of other denominations befriended me. All of these people seemed
so incredibly beautiful and dedicated to Christ, and, might I say,
appeared to be much better parents than I was. I began to wonder
how these wonderful people with their differing religious beliefs
could all be going to hell, as the Baptists had taught me. This made
no sense to me. This thought blew me away!

I visited Buddhist and Shinto temples. I explored the island. The Okinawan people weren't heathen, as the Baptists had forewarned me. Their beauty and their generosity touched me. My mind exploded. It was a moment of truth that changed me forever. I didn't know it at the time, but upon my return to the United States I would become a spiritual "seeker." My religious experience in Okinawa left me thirsting for a spiritual atmosphere that would be inclusive rather than exclusive.

The second thing that changed my life in Okinawa was a decision to perform on stage. My husband observed that I was "doing better" when I was performing. I believe that "doing better" meant having a creative outlet that relieved my sadness and anxiety. With this creative outlet came more freedom; but because of my dark side, I couldn't safely handle that much freedom.

In Okinawa I began attracting the kind of men who could really hurt me. This was during the Vietnam War in the mid-1960s, when many people were testing the limits of conventional morality. I entered into superficial relationships that were extremely risky. Every risk carried a thrill, but it also carried a consequence. I was headed for a real downhill slide if I didn't pull back and stop this behavior. Yet even though I was becoming conscious of the risks I was taking, I didn't know how to stop what I was doing.

I was growing more calculating and developing a hardness of heart with each risk I took. With each risk there came a growing fear, but it was as if I were still a little girl seeking the power of my father's attention, the only power I really wanted. I was far from knowing then what I have come now to understand. I later came to understand that this yearning for my father's attention was really a deep spiritual longing for a connection with the true, ultimate source of authority—God. But it would be a long time before I would understand how these wayward yearnings were part of a greater process that was propelling me forward in my own spiritual pathway.

First Encounter with the Bahá'í Faith

When my husband's tour of duty in Okinawa ended in 1967, we returned to the United States, settling in the Dallas area. We began to search for a new church because we did not want to return to the narrow world of traditional Christian worship. We sampled Theosophy, Rosicrucianism, and other faith traditions. My husband was offered a job in my hometown of Rockford, Illinois, and we moved there in 1968, still searching for a religion that was compatible with our beliefs. We began attending both Jewish and Unitarian services.

We first learned of the Bahá'í Faith in 1969 through a newspaper announcement regarding an upcoming informational event at the home of a Bahá'í couple. I was apprehensive as my husband and I approached the door to their home, but my fears were swept away by the warmth and love I found inside. As they spoke of the Bahá'í teachings, I knew that this was the inclusive faith I had been looking for. The Bahá'í Faith encouraged me to ask questions and seek the truth for myself. They called this the principle of independent investigation of the truth. This was probably the most threatening principle I could ever try to incorporate into my own life. It would take years for me to fully absorb the potential of this one principle.

I imagine everyone who comes to the Bahá'í Faith brings his or her own set of problems. We can't foresee how the Faith is going to change our lives. We cannot yet conceive of the real power to heal that is embedded in the Bahá'í scriptures. I believe it was through God's grace and bounty that I recognized Bahá'u'lláh, the Prophet and Founder of the Bahá'í Faith, as the Messenger of God for today. I knew I was on a self-destructive path, wandering and stumbling around blindly from one dangerous situation to another. The Bahá'í Faith seemed like a point of light on the path to a new way of life. I declared my belief in Bahá'u'lláh and became a member of the religion.

I made friends as a new Bahá'í. I taught what I was learning to others. For two years I studied the Faith, and I was moved by the spiritual truths I discovered—especially the principle of the independent investigation of truth. This principle is intimately linked to the principle of justice. My heart leapt when I read in the Bahá'í scriptures,

> O Son of Spirit!
> The best beloved of all things in My sight is Justice; turn not away therefrom if thou desirest me, and neglect it not that I may confide in thee. By its aid thou shalt see with thine own eyes and not through the eyes of others, and shalt know of thine own knowledge and not through the knowledge of thy neighbor. Ponder this in thy heart; how it behoveth thee to be. Verily justice is My gift to thee and the sign of My loving-kindness. Set it then before thine eyes.[3]

Justice: A Core Concept

Justice is the greatest thing in the eyes of God! This was new and startling information for me. I had always heard "God is love" and "Love your neighbor as yourself." I had wrestled over and over again in my mind with the issue of how to love those who oppressed me. How could I rid myself of this hatred? How could I love all that tyranny? How could I respond with anything but rage and a desire to hurt others after all that I had been through? After having been sexually abused at the hands of my father, the most important authority figure in my life, it was extremely difficult for me to conceive of God, the ultimate authority figure, as just and loving. Yet as I began to explore the history and teachings of the Bahá'í Faith, I learned that Bahá'u'lláh had suffered tremendously at the hands of his oppressors. I learned that even in the times of his greatest suffering, he had also experienced great joy and radiated such love that those who came in contact with him were transformed spiritually. I began to see that if it was possible for him to transcend his suffering, which was much greater than my own, then maybe it was possible for me to transcend my difficulties too.

I began to see that my own life needed what religion had to offer, namely a reason for existence that reached beyond the limits of my own small life. I began to see myself as part of a grander scheme of things, a scheme that originated when time began and will stretch into eternity.

The suffering that I had endured began to take on a new meaning. This new understanding propelled me to seek my spiritual core. I began to see that my suffering helped me appreciate that religion was not a "one-day-a-week" event tacked onto life but the very core, the very center of life itself. I turned to God out of desperation and found what I believe to be the latest of the revelations in God's ongoing relationship with creation. I found the Bahá'í revelation.

2

Searching for
Spiritual Identity

During early adulthood my life had become a mass of confusion as a result of all my trials and sufferings, my sexual acting out, and my painful self-hatred. The first glimmer of hope for me was to discover that religious truth could be my salvation. In particular, the Bahá'í Faith, with its emphasis on its "twin pillars" of justice and love, attracted me to its wisdom. I began to study the religion and soon discovered one of my most beloved books of scripture, the Seven Valleys.

The Seven Valleys was written by the Prophet and Founder of the Bahá'í Faith, Bahá'u'lláh. The book was originally written in the form of a letter responding to questions posed by a Muslim judge in Persia. In it Bahá'u'lláh describes the stages of spiritual growth and development. He explains that spiritual progress, like all progress in life, is developmental. It proceeds through stages, one building upon the next, each possessing its own character, challenges, and acquired wisdom.

The concept of spiritual development is similar in some ways to working with children. When I work with children and teach them to express themselves using the arts, I don't begin with complicated things like oil painting and sculpture. I begin simply, with things that are easy for them, and then we work our way up to the harder things. They begin with crayons, pencils, finger paints, and so forth. Then slowly, gradually, as they become comfortable with one medium, we gradually move on to the more difficult things such as oil painting and sculpture.

Bahá'u'lláh tells us in the Seven Valleys that we, too, must start simply in our own spiritual quest and that we have to work our way up. How do we begin? We start by searching, by seeking our own way, looking for truth. We remain our own authority, but in contrast to chapter 1, where my own authority was completely without aim or guidance and was just as likely to lead me astray as to lead

me forward, this new sense of personal authority is guided by a
search for truth. This journey has a purpose and a direction. Its
purpose is to perfect our characters and bring us closer and closer to
God. Its direction is toward goodness and away from things that
are not beneficial.

The journey is not easy for anyone, much less for someone who
begins with traumatic injuries sustained as a result of childhood
sexual abuse, as I did. The experiences I had undergone with my
father confused the good with the bad. The one who loved me had
also hurt me. The one who was supposed to protect me had injured
me. The one who was supposed to train and guide me had told me
all sorts of things that were false and even harmful. No wonder I
was confused. I found life to be so difficult that sometimes I could
barely cope. At times it was hard not to give up.

Patience

Bahá'u'lláh encourages us and tells us not to give up on our search
for spiritual truth, no matter what may happen. I quote him here,
again from the Seven Valleys:

The Valley of Search
    The steed of this Valley is patience; without patience the way-
farer on this journey will reach nowhere and attain no goal. Nor
should he ever be downhearted; if he strive for a hundred thousand years and yet fail to behold the beauty of the Friend, he
should not falter. For those who seek the Ka'bih* of "for Us"

_____

* The holy sanctuary at Mecca. Here the word means "goal."

rejoice in the tidings: "In Our ways will we guide them." In their search, they have stoutly girded up the loins of service, and seek at every moment to journey from the plane of heedlessness into the realm of being. No bond shall hold them back, and no counsel shall deter them.[1]

I first read these words many years ago, and to this day, I still love to read them over and over. In so short and succinct a grouping of words, Bahá'u'lláh has outlined the task of life. He says first of all to have patience and never to be "downhearted." Oh, how I needed to hear and heed this advice! Nothing is harder for me than patience with myself. I realize that my experiences left me with scars and wounds that need to heal, and yet I have trouble being patient while this slow healing process unfolds. Bahá'u'lláh says we should never be downhearted and never give up, even if we strive "for a hundred thousand years"!

Striving

So patience is the first thing Bahá'u'lláh says we require in our spiritual search for truth. The second thing is striving. Striving, what does that mean? It means to set your sights on something and make an effort. It means to aim—to have a purpose. The Bible says, "For where your treasure is, there will your heart be also." In other words, if you are seeking to draw closer to God, you can't also be seeking things that are the opposite of God. "Ye cannot serve God and mammon," the Bible says.[2] You have to make a choice about what you are doing with your life. For me, stopping to think about this made a real difference.

We are told in the Bahá'í writings that the search for truth has to be completely wholehearted: "The state in which one should be to seriously search for the truth is the condition of the thirsty, burning soul desiring the water of life, of the fish struggling to reach sea, of the sufferer seeking the true doctor to obtain the divine cure, of the lost caravan endeavoring to find the right road, of the lost and wandering ship striving to reach the shore of salvation."[3]

So if we want to find the truth we must find the road to the Divine Physician who can help heal and guide us. We have to make this quest our first priority. We have to strive, and if we do, Bahá'u'lláh promises that we will be guided. He says, "'In Our ways will we guide them.'"[4]

Paranoia and the Temporary Loss of My Reasoning Powers

Even though the Bahá'í Faith immediately began to bring a greater sense of peace and direction to my life as I began to explore its teachings and read its scriptures, my healing journey from this point forward was anything but smooth and peaceful. After I joined the Bahá'í Faith, I began to perform onstage again. Once again I found myself beginning to slide downhill. I was out of control! My highs were extremely high, and my lows were extremely low. I began to pull away from my husband and be drawn to out-of-control sexual behavior.

This type of sickness, this type of immorality cannot be wished or prayed away. It's not a matter of willpower. I believe everyone who comes to the Bahá'í Faith brings his or her own set of problems. We cannot foresee how our lives are going to change. We cannot conceive of the healing power that lies within the Bahá'í scriptures or the real interest that Bahá'u'lláh devotes to us as individuals. I believe it was through God's grace and bounty that I recognized Bahá'u'lláh as the Messenger of God for today. For two years I studied the Bahá'í Faith, and I was moved by the spiritual truths I discovered. I began to teach others what I was learning. I was especially moved and impressed—as I have mentioned—by the principle of individual investigation of truth. This principle implies the right and responsibility to ask questions, which at that time was beyond my ability.

And then rather suddenly, in the short four-month period between October 1971 and January 1972, several very traumatic events occurred. I got a divorce; I put my aged, loyal dog to sleep; and my father, my abuser, died of lung cancer at age fifty-three. I had dearly loved my dog, I had taken care of my father during the last weeks of his life, and my husband was probably the best friend I had ever had in my life. Considering my emotional instability at the time, even one of these extremely stressful events could very well have caused me to lose my balance. I was completely overwhelmed.

I did not cry. I did not feel anything. I went into a trancelike state in which I heard voices. The voices said, "Give everything away." I asked, "Where should I start?" The reply was "Start with the kitchen table." I said, "Of course, none of it is mine anyway!"

Slowly, methodically, one trip at a time, I loaded up the trunk and backseat of my 1968 black Dodge Dart. I gave everything away— beds, stereos, bookshelves, knock-down furniture, pots, pans, and blankets—to Bahá'ís, neighbors, hippies, and strangers. It was a Herculean effort for one very weak woman. However, in what I later came to recognize as a manic state, I was capable of doing almost anything. (In 1999, after many years of being misdiagnosed and taking the wrong medication, I was diagnosed with bipolar disorder.)

When I finished giving away all of my possessions, I went across the street to a neighbor. She took me into her arms and rocked me and crooned to me. It was a quiet moment of rest after a very busy day. But it was also a moment to nurture the child within me who could neither look to the future, nor understand the consequences of her actions, nor even the reasons behind them, because her emotional growth had been stunted. I had no thought of the future. I felt only a quiet trust.

My children slept at my neighbor's home that night. I went back to my empty house and lay down on the carpet in my bedroom. I went into a trance again, and in my trance the voice said, "The police are going to come and get you now." The doorbell rang, and I went downstairs to open the door. The police were there, so I let them in. I had no fear, I felt no need or desire to resist. They took me to a mental health facility.

When I awoke the next day, I was in terror! My deepest fear had come to pass: I was locked up! I was no longer in a trance. This was a harsh reality! My bizarre behavior had been reported to the authorities. For seven days I pretended to be as normal as possible and did my best to explain my behavior. I refused medication. I refused to admit that anything was wrong with me. When that didn't persuade the authorities to release me, I became totally resistant to treatment. I perceived everything and everyone as a threat to me. I was afraid that if I took any medicine I would lose control and wouldn't be able to defend myself if I were attacked. I refused to drink from the drinking fountain, thinking they had put medicine in it. Terror and anxiety compelled me to roam the halls continually reciting the Lord's Prayer. I was terrified that someone would attack me while I was sleeping. I forced myself to remain awake as long as I could. After brief periods of sleep I would awaken in a state of panic as wave after wave of adrenalin washed over me.

Choice Is Possible

Eventually I was released from the hospital and I began a long period of struggle during which I was sometimes in a rational state of mind and sometimes not. My behavior did not immediately fall into line. I mentioned in chapter 1 that I had been engaging in many behaviors that I felt conflicted about. I was acting out all kinds of impulses, desires, and passions. I felt guilty, maybe, but I continued to do things I knew were wrong anyway. I felt compelled.

But, compelled by past experiences or not, after reading the Seven Valleys in more depth, I began to realize that I always had a choice. I always had a choice to try to turn to God or to just turn away from Him and act without really thinking things through. I began to realize that when I at least exerted the effort to make the right choices and keep my life turning to God, the effort itself brought me strength and encouragement in ways that were amazing. I slowly began to realize that by making these efforts to have patience and strive and choose what is good for me, I was beginning to unleash a whole host of spiritual powers I didn't even know I had! The important thing was to keep trying even though I felt I was failing over and over again. The important thing was to keep my "eye on the ball" and keep paying attention to my actions and the question of whether or not they were leading me in the right direction.

I found at first that it was very hard to keep trying because so many of my behaviors and thought processes seemed "automatic." Sometimes I would even say or do things and then wonder, "Why did I say that?" or "Why did I do that?" It was as if certain parts of me were taking over when I wasn't really paying attention.

As I continued to learn about spiritual qualities, I realized that this issue of attention is a key to spiritual growth and development.

The Power of Attention

In the writings of Bahá'u'lláh, the power of attention is often connected to our sense of hearing or our "inner ear," which seems to indicate a connection to the power of intuition and the Holy Spirit. He writes, "Blind thine eyes . . . to all save My beauty; stop thine ears to all save My word; empty thyself of all learning save the knowledge of Me; that with a clear vision, a pure heart and an attentive ear thou mayest enter the court of My holiness."[5]

The power of attention is a power of applying the mind and observant powers to the tasks of learning lessons and serving God. It is a state of being alert to and discerning of every aspect of each situation one faces, all the while searching for the spiritual direction in that situation. The Buddhist text known as the Dhammapada states, "Foolish, ignorant people indulge in careless lives, whereas a clever man guards his attention as his most precious possession." 'Abdu'l-Bahá, the son and successor of Bahá'u'lláh, is credited with saying, "There is a wonderful power and strength which belongs to the human spirit, but it must receive confirmation from the Holy Spirit. But if it is aided by the Bounty of the Holy Spirit, it will show great power; it will discover realities; it will be informed of the mysteries. Direct all the attention to the Holy Spirit, and call the attention of every soul to it. Then you will see wonderful signs."[6]

Finding a New Spiritual Identity

The early days of my spiritual awakening were a time of joy and amazement, but they were also a time of crisis and confusion. As I slowly, doggedly, and sometimes unevenly tried to turn away from old habits and ways of thinking, I realized that I needed to make more than just a few superficial changes. I needed a complete overhaul. It was like thinking at first that your car needs a tune-up only to find out that it needs not only a new engine but a total restoration. The more honestly I looked at myself the more I realized I needed a whole new sense of what life was about and what I was about. I needed, in a sense, a new identity.

Identity is being yourself and not someone else. It is the fact that you exist as a separate entity, expressing self-identity, and that you, as a single human being, are distinguished from others on the basis of your own attributes. It is acting according to your true self, without hypocrisy or constraint. Your sense of identity gives you the ability to know firmly who you are, what is important to you, what you think is right and wrong, and where you fit into this world. It enables you to know where your identity ends and the identities of your parents, spouse, children, friends, and others begin, so that you do not enmesh yourself in someone else's identity or allow others to enmesh themselves in yours.

The Dual Nature of Man

As I continued to study the Bahá'í Faith, I learned that the issue of personal identity is complicated by the fact that there are two sides to human nature. 'Abdu'l-Bahá explains,

In man there are two natures; his spiritual or higher nature and his material or lower nature. In one he approaches God, in the other he lives for the world alone. Signs of both these natures are to be found in men. In his material aspect he expresses untruth,

cruelty and injustice; all these are the outcome of his lower nature. The attributes of his Divine nature are shown forth in love,
mercy, kindness, truth and justice, one and all being expressions
of his higher nature. Every good habit, every noble quality belongs to man's spiritual nature, whereas all his imperfections and
sinful actions are born of his material nature.[7]

When I read this statement about the two natures of man, it was
as if a light bulb went on inside my head. This statement explained
what I had been feeling. It was as if a fight were going on inside me
between two sides of myself—one part wanting one thing, another
part wanting another. I had always thought that this fighting inside
me was only because of my history of abuse. I didn't know that this
kind of internal conflict was part of everyone's life! I felt so grateful
for this new understanding, and that gratitude led me logically to a
new spiritual power, the power of understanding.

The Power of Understanding

The power of understanding enables you to grasp the nature,
significance, or explanation of something; to comprehend; and to
make experience intelligible by applying concepts and categories,
arriving at a result after being informed or educated or through the
process of consultation. Bahá'u'lláh writes,

First and foremost among these favors, which the Almighty hath
conferred upon man, is the gift of understanding. His purpose
in conferring such a gift is none other except to enable His creatures to know and recognize the one true God—exalted be His
glory. This gift giveth man the power to discern the truth in all

things, leadeth him to that which is right, and helpeth him to discover the secrets of creation.[8]

The Power of Thought and Reasoning

The power of understanding leads to a deeper understanding of the power of thought and its relationship to action. 'Abdu'l-Bahá informs us that "The reality of man is his thought, not his material body." He said, "The illumination of the Holy Spirit gives to man the power of thought, and enables him to make discoveries by which he bends the laws of nature to his will."[9]

The power of thought is the action or process of thinking and the formation and arrangement of ideas in the mind. It is an idea suggested or recalled, a reflection or consideration, an opinion or judgment, a belief or supposition with which to then reason, reflect upon, understand, act upon, or discard. Many who have been traumatized, especially women, are afraid to reveal or speak their thoughts and opinions. This hinders the development of their identity and paralyzes their power to respond and act.

Reason involves evaluating experiences and drawing conclusions. This process includes the right and the opportunity to discuss your own thoughts and point of view—including facts, interpretation of facts, and your values—in two-way dialogue or consultation, and in this way become informed, educated, and empowered to discover reality. Only by reasoning aloud, without fear of punishment or threats, can children and adults develop a strong sense of identity and benefit from guidance and support. 'Abdu'l-Bahá states, "Know ye that God has created in man the power of reason, whereby man is enabled to investigate reality."[10]

Investigating Reality

To investigate reality, as 'Abdu'l-Bahá mentions, is a process of trying to discover new information about oneself and one's spiritual journey. It is a process of uncovering the hidden talents and powers latent inside your spiritual nature. The Bahá'í writings call these talents and powers the "Hidden Mysteries" latent in the soul. To discover is to obtain knowledge, to arrive through search or study at new knowledge, and to be the first to find, to learn, or to observe. 'Abdu'l-Bahá says,

> God has given man the eye of investigation by which he may see and recognize truth. He has endowed man with ears that he may hear the message of reality and conferred upon him the gift of reason by which he may discover things for himself. This is his endowment and equipment for the investigation of reality. Man is not intended to see through the eyes of another, hear through another's ears nor comprehend with another's brain. Each human creature has individual endowment, power and responsibility in the creative plan of God. Therefore, depend upon your own reason and judgment and adhere to the outcome of your own investigation; otherwise, you will be utterly submerged in the sea of ignorance and deprived of the bounties of God.[11]

The power of intellectual investigation of truth confirms and validates the power of inner vision. Investigation of reality dispels darkness, curtails imitation, and helps to create unity. This faculty allows us to observe and inquire in detail, to examine systematically, and to search. It enables us to examine things closely in the quest for information or truth. Bahá'ís know this power by a more common name—the independent investigation of truth.

Independent Investigation of Truth

Regarding independent investigation of the truth, 'Abdu'l-Bahá writes,

God has conferred upon and added to man a distinctive power, the faculty of intellectual investigation into the secrets of creation, the acquisition of higher knowledge, the greatest virtue of which is scientific enlightenment.

This endowment is the most praiseworthy power of man, for through its employment and exercise, the betterment of the human race is accomplished, the development of the virtues of mankind is made possible and the spirit and mysteries of God become manifest.[12]

Elsewhere 'Abdu'l-Bahá says, "Ponder and reflect: All sciences, arts, crafts, inventions and discoveries, have been once the secrets of nature and in conformity with the laws thereof must remain hidden; yet man through his discovering power interfereth with the laws of nature and transfereth these hidden secrets from the invisible to the visible plane."[13]

To experience the power of discovery, we have to assert our right to ask questions (the power of intellectual investigation of truth), and we have to develop the cognitive power, which may have been denied us. The root of the power of discovery is the power of understanding, or the intellect, of which 'Abdu'l-Bahá has said, "the intellect . . . is supernatural. Through intellectual and intelligent inquiry science is the discoverer of all things. It unites present and past, reveals the history of bygone nations and events, and confers upon man today the essence of all human knowledge and attainment throughout the ages. By intellectual processes and logical deductions of reason this superpower in man can penetrate the mysteries of the future and anticipate its happenings."[14]

The Power of Reflection

Another closely related power is the power of reflection, which is the power to think or to consider seriously, usually in a meditative or pensive state. It is the concentration of the mind and the results of such concentration, communicated or not. Those who are hypervigilant are deprived of the power of reflection. If blind obedience has been exacted from us, we may be afraid to develop the power of reflection. Some people who have been traumatized escape the meditative state and fall into a trance, which is called *dissociation*. Those for whom this is a problem need to develop the ability to consciously stay in the meditative state. 'Abdu'l-Bahá says that "conscious reflection" is a power belonging to man. Bahá'u'lláh writes, "The source of crafts, sciences and arts is the power of reflection. Make ye every effort that out of this ideal mine there may gleam forth such pearls of wisdom and utterance as will promote the well-being and harmony of all the kindreds of the earth."[15]

Bahá'u'lláh says there is a sign from God in every phenomenon: the sign of the intellect is contemplation and the sign of contemplation is silence, because it is impossible for a man to do two things at one time—he cannot both speak and meditate.

The Powers of Induction and Deduction

Induction is reasoning from the particular to the general—to infer by inductive reasoning. It is to draw a conclusion based on observation of particular instances and may also be based on emotions, memories, inner vision, intellectual investigation of truth, and reasoning. One example of inductive reasoning that could be truth or fantasy is as follows: "Mom has been drinking alcohol. Mom is very angry right now. Based on these observations, past experiences, and the feelings of dread and fear I am having right now, I had better stay out of her path. Better yet, I'll disappear." 'Abdu'l-Bahá refers to the power of induction, writing, "Also he [man] bringeth to light the past events that have been lost to memory, and forseeth by his power of induction future happenings that are as yet unknown."[16]

The word "induce" means to lead a person by persuasion—or some influence or motive that acts upon the power of will—and thereby facilitate change in behavior, attitude, condition, belief, or opinion. The persuasion, influence, or motive that acts on the will is a power called "principle," which defines truth and thus infers correct action for the individual and society. This is how all of the spiritual principles in Bahá'u'lláh's revelation act upon the will of humankind to precipitate solutions to social problems.

Deduction is the opposite of induction; it is reasoning from the general to the particular. 'Abdu'l-Bahá wrote of deduction in regard to the power of discovery, "By intellectual processes and logical deductions of reason this superpower in man can penetrate the mysteries of the future and anticipate its happenings."[17] There are times when a woman might be condemned by a man for not being "logical," which may result either from not being trained in inductive and deductive reasoning or from having her attempts discounted.

Discernment and the Powers of the Mind

From this short list of just some of the spiritual powers of the mind available to all of us, we see that the ability to discern truth from error is central to the process of spiritual development. Our choices about our own behavior are dependent upon our analysis of what is true and what is not true, what is guidance from God and what is not, and upon the value of the advice in our own lives. The Bahá'í writings refer to the ability to weed out truth from error and sort through conflicting opinions in search of truth as the power of discernment.

However, when an individual is denied the facts, given false information, or simply denied the opportunity to make any choices, he or she is unable to develop the power of discernment. So the power of discernment is related to, and dependent upon, the power of intellectual investigation of truth. The power of discernment is also dependent upon the power of understanding and the cognitive power. We have to know and understand why something is right or wrong. Bahá'u'lláh has written the following verse in one of His most powerful tablets: "Verily this is that Most Great Beauty, foretold in the Books of the Messengers, through Whom truth shall be distinguished from error and the wisdom of every command shall be tested."[18] I like to think of the tablet as a prayer for discernment.

3

Turning to the Light

In chapters 1 and 2, I explained how sexual and emotional abuse had rendered me powerless as a child. As a result of the abuse, I had become lost and confused. Life became even more difficult when I lapsed into a state of complete irrationality—a state of mind mental health professionals call psychosis. Finding the Bahá'í Faith gave me a new understanding of myself. I began a spiritual journey that opened my eyes to a new way of life. As this journey began to unfold, my study of Bahá'í scripture taught me that I possessed an untold wealth of spiritual resources that had been completely hidden from me. As I studied more and more, these spiritual resources would become my foundation. I was beginning to learn step by step how to mine the gems within that had been placed there by a loving Creator.

Among the hardest things for me to realize was that understanding the scriptures and yearning for a relationship with God was not enough to bring about the changes I wanted. I came to the awareness that, in addition to discovering all the spiritual gifts I had been given, I now had to begin making an effort to conform my behavior to the will of God if I wanted to progress. Our Creator would not have granted power to us without also setting limits and boundaries for those powers. If we go beyond those limits, we will not only lose our psychological balance, but we will also lose our spiritual balance. We will suffer a loss of tranquillity. In essence, the laws of God as expressed in the revelation of Bahá'u'lláh are the boundaries or limits that He has set for us today. I began to see the difficulty of getting on a spiritual pathway and staying on it. I encountered many obstacles, the first of which was the idea that I had to be perfect to be a Bahá'í.

Feeling Unworthy

When I first began to realize there was a huge discrepancy between the standard of conduct prescribed by Bahá'u'lláh and the way I was living my own life, I felt totally overwhelmed. In fact, not realizing that spiritual development was an incremental process, I condemned myself as unworthy to be or to call myself a Bahá'í. I believed Bahá'u'lláh was the Messenger of God for today, and I loved the Bahá'í Faith so much that I mistakenly believed I was protecting the religion by withdrawing from it. I believed that my behavior would somehow damage the Faith, and I didn't want to do that. This was the beginning of a period of ten years during which I ostracized myself from the Bahá'í Faith because I felt I had to protect people from my depravity. During this self-imposed banishment, I prayed that Bahá'u'lláh would heal me. I prayed for celibacy, and I prayed for chastity of mind.

I didn't realize then what I know now. I thought I had to withdraw from the Faith because I wasn't good enough. I didn't realize that the whole purpose of the Bahá'í Faith is to help us along on our spiritual journey and that it doesn't matter where that spiritual journey begins. The journey is never ending. It begins with the recognition of Bahá'u'lláh as the Messenger of God for this day. When one recognizes him and begins to understand who he is, one begins to have the desire to act according to his guidance. But spiritual development is not an instantaneous process. I had years and years of old habits to overcome. I had to completely change my understanding of myself and my own identity. This kind of change takes time. It involves a process of growth, and all growth takes time.

During my ten-year period of self-imposed exile, I imagined myself to be far away from God, but nothing could be further from the truth. During this time, as I continued to struggle with sexual acting out and other behaviors that baffled and confused me, I was nonetheless developing my ability to conduct an independent search for truth. This required that I learn to talk, to ask questions, and to be aware.

The Dual Nature of Man

As we discussed in chapter 2, I learned as I began to study the Bahá'í Faith that there are two sides to human nature—our spiritual or "higher" nature and our lower or "material" nature. Our spiritual nature is inclined toward God, and our lower nature is attracted to the material world. It was a revelation to me to discover that *both* natures were within me. Even though I was struggling mightily to control my darker side, or my material nature—sometimes successfully and sometimes not so successfully—I still had a spiritual nature.

Uncovering the Dark Side

However, before I could begin to heal, it was vital that I become fully conscious of the lower, dark side of me so that I could hold myself accountable for all of my actions. That process proved to be a trauma in its own right, because it meant that I would have to confront the sexually obsessed part of me that had been formed during six dark years of childhood sexual abuse. This was a painful process.

The darker side of me seemed to have been arrested in her development at the age of eight or younger. She was raw. She would not take "no" for an answer. She was repulsive, vulgar, full of rage, perverted, depraved, and only minimally verbal. She had delusions of grandeur and power, and she was uncontrollable. She had no fear of God, she was shameless, and she was me.

At the age of thirty in the summer of 1971, I unexpectedly caught a glimpse of this darker side of me when I was telling a male acquaintance—a musician—about a man with whom I thought I was in love. We were sitting in his car after we had performed at a local night spot. He asked, "How do you know you love him?" I said in a strange, tiny voice that sounded like a very little girl, "I can't tell you, but I can show you." He looked at me intently for a moment, then pulled back and said, "My God! Your lips are swollen and you look like an animal!" Who was this strange person who created such revulsion in others and shame in me? Praise God, I was finally conscious of her presence!

I did not know that I was going to recognize the presence of this other facet of my identity. I could not understand it. But a quotation from Bahá'u'lláh now comes to mind: "Liberty causeth man to overstep the bounds of propriety, and to infringe on the dignity of his station. It debaseth him to the level of extreme depravity and wickedness."[1] The darker side of me—my lower nature—did not know that there were bounds of propriety. How could she? She had been created in the dark by someone who had taken liberty with God's creation and had perverted it. Because of her age and because her normal development had been interrupted, she could not be expected to control her sexuality.

My conditioning as a young child had been in direct conflict with the revelation of Bahá'u'lláh, and it certainly placed me in the position of being viewed as "evil" in the traditional Christian understanding of the concept. However, as the following quotation reveals, children must be taught the laws of God to enable them to have strong boundaries and a healthy fear of God that will motivate them to strive toward moral behavior. Concerning the education of children, Bahá'u'lláh writes,

That which is of paramount importance for the children, that which must precede all else, is to teach them the oneness of God and the laws of God. For lacking this, the fear of God cannot be inculcated, and lacking the fear of God an infinity of odious and abominable actions will spring up and sentiments will be uttered that transgress all bounds. . . .[2]

Though I could not articulate such questions at the time, when I became conscious of my darker side, I wondered if there was any hope of reforming this darker side of me by learning the laws of God. I wondered if I was permanently perverted. Was I capable of learning new behavior? Would I ever be able to overcome the sexually obsessed darker side of me?

In late 1972 I started attending a nonsectarian church. I wrote a story titled *Skylark, the Bird Who Learned to Fly,* which was about a bird that had been abused in the nest. Skylark decided that he wasn't supposed to fly. Another bird named Dovie taught Skylark that he could fly if he took responsibility for his life. Enlisting the help of the children in the church, I created puppets and produced the play for a Sunday morning presentation in the spring of 1973. I was exhilarated when my Skylark puppet, aided by a tiny screw at the top of his head and a fishing pole at the side of the church, flew into the audience at the end of the play, yelling, "I can fly! I can fly! I can flyyyyyyyyyyy!"

Turning to the Light

With the success of my puppet show about Skylark, I began to feel a little more equal with others. Feeling equal was very important to me. I decided to talk to the minister of the church about what I was going through, thinking that such counseling would be preferable to psychotherapy. This turned out to be a mistake.

When I sought counseling with the minister, he tried to seduce me. Then he gave me a book entitled *Open Marriage* to read. I knew instantly that this was not what I wanted or needed. I left the minister's home in a state of intense anxiety, and I decided to leave the church. Had I somehow unwittingly invited the minister's attempt to seduce me? I didn't know if what had happened was my fault, but I couldn't be sure! All I knew was that I didn't feel safe, so I moved on. Although this was a very unsettling experience that led me to doubt myself, it was nonetheless a sign of growth because I had made a healthy choice in rejecting the minister's unwanted advances. This was progress, painful as it was.

I wanted very much to sing professionally and had sung in nightclubs and churches off and on from an early age. Singing gave my soul release, but it also felt dangerous and threatening because it was linked to sensuality and my dark side. Sometimes while singing I felt more like a sexualized person than a vocalist who was dedicated to her craft. The following is a painful excerpt from my journal, illustrating the conflict between the person I wanted to be and the dark side of me who inhabited the deepest chasms of my mind:

> Don't sing! Singing attracts people to me. To sing would be the greatest expression of my sexuality. I am not sexual. I do not have sexual needs. Other people do but I don't. I want nothing to do with sex. Sex is evil. All of these problems I'm having, the break-up of my marriage, my acting out, everything is happening because I wanted to sing professionally. I feel threatened when I sing because I feel sexual and I make people think sexual thoughts. I feel like I'm going to lose control. What are these strange feelings in my abdomen? I don't want these feelings. They scare me! If I sing, I will become promiscuous. People will find out that I am evil!

This thought process was repeated whenever I faced a moral choice, particularly if it was related to sex, as it often was. Being confronted with the need to make a decision would set off an anxiety attack. All choices terrified me, regardless of whether they concerned something important or something inconsequential. Even a decision to do something as simple as go to the grocery store was difficult. I felt as if I truly did not know myself, and I did not want to know the part of me that was connected to the sexually obsessed child. I never knew what that part of me might do, and I wanted to be sure to do the right thing.

Everyone Has the Same Issue

It is relevant to note here that the Bahá'í concept of good and evil, while similar to that of other religions, differs in two important ways.

First, Bahá'u'lláh exhorts us to bring ourselves to account on a daily basis. He writes,

O SON OF BEING!
Bring thyself to account each day ere thou art summoned to a reckoning; for death, unheralded, shall come upon thee and thou shalt be called to give account for thy deeds.[3]

This implies that each of us is personally responsible for our own behavior and that the choices we make from day to day and moment to moment are important. Because we have a spiritual side and a darker, material side, the choices we make can support the development of either side.

Second, good and evil are not black-and-white all-or-nothing concepts that condemn mental illness, ignorance, innocence, imperfection, weakness, and such. Earlier I stated that we are all involved in a process of spiritual development, striving toward perfection. God knew my weakness and knew what experiences would help me grow. Bahá'u'lláh writes, "None can escape the snares He setteth, and no soul can find release except through submission to His will."[4] I believe He sometimes set the snare, or tested me, with another person, whom He knew intimately, who had the same weakness, so that both of us would experience an expansion of consciousness, or spiritual growth. That is His mercy. I experienced the consequences of my own actions again and again until I achieved expansion of consciousness. Over time, with practice, I was able to change my habits and steer myself away from choices that reflected the dark side to habitual choices that aligned my thoughts and behavior with the teachings of Bahá'u'lláh. This was the healing power of obedience to God.

Trusting That Your Trials and Tribulations Have Meaning

Although at times I became discouraged with my own seeming lack of progress, I had to trust that God was providing lessons to expand my consciousness because He thought I was capable of understanding and because He wanted to use me in a greater capacity. Indeed, He leads us to trust during tribulation with the following verse from a Bahá'í prayer: "I know of a certainty, by virtue of My love for Thee, that Thou wilt never cause tribulations to befall any soul unless Thou desirest to exalt his station in Thy celestial Paradise."[5] The expansion of consciousness led me to new perceptions.

New perceptions led to new choices. The increasing stability of my chaste volition became the foundation for a greater expansion of consciousness.

Often our greatest challenges lie within us. Our life experiences engage the things inside us that need to change. As we work out what for us are trials and tribulations, our spiritual nature untangles itself from the snares of our dark side. As we wrestle with our problems, our reliance on God is increased. We turn to Him in prayer and ask for strength to overcome the obstacle. This process itself transforms us. This is the process of spiritual development; therefore it is the process of life itself. It is the process of learning about and nurturing our true nature, the nature that reflects the beauty and goodness of God.

Our beliefs emerge for us to witness in our actions. It is then that we compare our beliefs to God's Word. This is why we are called to bring ourselves to account each day by scrutinizing our actions. Exposure to the Word of God shows us where our beliefs and thought processes need correction. Often the sense of being off track is accompanied by a feeling of shame. Shame, while uncomfortable, can be a valuable ally in our search for spiritual direction. It is a spiritual "alarm" signaling us to examine our actions closely and be sure that we are following our chosen spiritual pathway.

Another word for following our spiritual pathway is "obedience." In this day and age, obedience has been given a bad name. But eventually I began to understand that obedience leads to psychological stability, and, conversely, disobedience leads to instability. The Bahá'í writings state that there are two kinds of healing: physical healing and spiritual healing. They explain that physical healing must be reinforced by spiritual healing, which is best obtained through obedience to the laws and commandments of God as revealed to us through His Messengers. Obedience, then, was going to be an important part of my healing.

4

Telling the Secret

The next facet of myself that I was to discover and direct was my emotions. In 1975, when my children were ages fourteen, twelve, and eleven, I enrolled in a parenting class at the YMCA because I felt I was a failure as a parent. In the absence of my former husband, I now raged at my oldest child. But the most astonishing thing occurred. One entire two-hour class session was devoted to teaching us about feelings. I clearly realized that I knew nothing about feelings. I recognized that I had been trying to prevent my children from feeling anger or sadness about my divorcing their father.

After the class, I went home and opened my manuscript, *Skylark, the Bird Who Learned to Fly*. I examined the pages, searching for words that expressed feelings. There were none. I had described conditions, actions, events, people, plot, thoughts, and characters, but there was no description of emotion. No feeling words had been used for Skylark to explain his emotional condition after years of abuse.

Before making this discovery, I would take out the manuscript every six months or so just to look at it and wonder what to do with it. But now I had something to reflect on deeply. I went to work rewriting the Skylark manuscript. This was great intellectual work for me, but I still could not feel my own emotions. However, this was a beginning; I was able at least to identify and match feelings to situations on paper and orally. Yet except for my rage and shame, which should have been examined in the context of the sexual abuse and directed at my father, I remained emotionally numb.

I painted ninety-seven watercolor illustrations for the Skylark story, recorded the narrative on audiotape, and turned it into a slide show. I began presenting programs for parents, nursing homes, schools, churches, and other groups. This boosted my self-esteem and feeling of equality as I timidly reentered society. As I taught others, I began to learn more, to tell more of my own story—though guardedly—and to internalize the concept of responsibility for oneself. This was quite an achievement after horrendous fear had driven me to the brink of destroying the work at least eight times over a period of six years. I thought this truth would destroy my family. I was terrified of my creativity; it led me to truth. The subconscious fear that I had was this: If I tell the truth about anything, I am in danger of telling the truth about the secret. I was terrified of my gifts; they led me to reveal my intelligence, and that was dangerous. I had learned very early in my family of origin that my intelligence had to be hidden. I dared not reveal that I had a different internal purpose or identity than others in my family did. I must have been gifted as a child, but one of my dearest sisters, when I began to reveal my gifts publicly, said in bewilderment, "Where is all of this coming from? How are you doing this?" She had no previous awareness of my potential.

It was also in 1975 that I began to be consumed by scatological thoughts that I found extremely distressing. I had thoughts of putting my face in feces, eating feces, smearing feces on my arms. These thoughts most often came up when I was singing at the Lutheran church I was attending at that time. The thoughts filled me with shame. How could I share this with anyone? I thought it was just one more thing that demonstrated how unworthy I was. People in the congregation would tell me how they had been moved to tears by the power of my singing, yet I could not enjoy it myself because of my distressing thoughts. Many years later in 1994 I shared this with my therapist. He told me that it sometimes happens to those who think they are unworthy of success. There was a part of myself that wanted to hurt my efforts toward success by flooding my mind with these scatological, obscene thoughts. I now know this was merely another symptom of the abuse I had suffered, but until I learned this, I hid these secret thoughts from everyone. (I was to experience these same thoughts again while singing in a magnificent chorus in New York City at the Bahá'í World Congress in 1992. Here I felt moved to the height of spirituality, with tears running down my face, but the beauty was marred by these horrible thoughts and by my self-condemnation for having them.)

I started dating the man who would eventually become my second husband in 1977. I had been aware that John was a member of my church for a long time, but I had always assumed he was married. When I attended a church retreat in a nearby city, I saw that he was placed in the singles group. After I found out that he was single, I invited him to my home for Sunday dinner. He refused my invitation. For about six months I invited him to dinner or a movie every couple of weeks, and still he continued to refuse. I prayed to God and decided that I was going to ask John one more time, and if he said no, I was going to look for another church to join, because there was no one else at the church I was interested in dating. I called John up one more time and he said no. I hung up the phone and said, "That's that!" However, John surprised me by calling back in twenty minutes and inviting me to a play. We dated for two years and married in 1979.

A Married Woman with a Dilemma

Now that I had spoken the vows of fidelity, I had a dilemma. I was still the same unhealed person who was acting out a pattern of seduction, easy familiarity, and availability. Even though I was married, there was still another man in my life with whom I was acting very provocatively, and there were others I was trying to attract. My anxiety about this situation was escalating. I knew I could not have it both ways, but I resisted engaging in ongoing therapy. I did not see a connection yet between my behavior and the sexual abuse I had suffered as a child.

Six months after John and I were married, I received a wonderful lesson in the form of a three-day marriage encounter weekend. During the weekend John and I shared many intense feelings. This was when I finally began to trust my spouse enough to tell him about the sexual abuse I had experienced as a child. I had not told him before because I thought he would reject me for being depraved and evil. I still feared that no man who knew the truth about my past would want me. I had fantasized that he would either leave me or have me locked up for being crazy. His supportive response surprised me. When I told him what had happened to me, he responded, "Now I understand why you wrote your Skylark story. I couldn't figure it out before; but now it fits." And at that point he began to offer me even more support than he had before. My faith increased dramatically! I had the acceptance of my husband, the person who was most dear to me. My desire to change deepened from that moment on.

The marriage encounter helped me to internalize the concepts about feelings that I had been learning. It was the first time that I had shared feelings openly and verbally with another human being, the first time I had felt truly heard by another human being, the first time I had truly listened to the feelings of another human being. It was an awakening!

However, something strange happened after the weekend of sharing feelings. I felt something wrong under the surface of my consciousness. I could find no words to express it. I ran into the bedroom. I tried to move my mouth, but it felt paralyzed. The closest I can come to describing the "something wrong" is that I thought my whole mind and body were going to explode. I opened my mouth, but nothing would come out. My throat constricted. I opened my mouth again, and an indescribable wounded sound was released. My husband came into the room and held me. I couldn't tell him what I was experiencing, but for the first time in my life, I did not feel alone. This was a monumental turning point for me. Someone was there to hold me, to mark this moment in time as different for me; it was a necessary step on my path toward wholeness. Being held there, then, was a moment of trust. I began to cry. I said, "John, I'm so afraid."

I thought, "What kind of fear is this?" I had felt fear before. I had experienced an adrenalin rush before. But this terror was something different. I came to believe that this was the same feeling of terror I had experienced as a very young child. I had been so young that I had not been able to express my fear and distress verbally. I was now fully conscious of the fear, the muteness, and the feeling of powerlessness. I was now able to reassure myself when I sensed the terror.

I attended a retreat at Augsburg College in Iowa. During communion at the altar of the chapel, a man from my church propositioned me. At the very altar of God! I felt as if I were no longer safe at church. I was ricocheting off the walls emotionally now! I was certain I had done nothing to encourage this man. I was bewildered.

I began to be consumed with what I call an awareness of blind fear. I would awaken at 1, 2, or 3 A.M. with anxiety attacks, not knowing why. Then I would just get back to sleep only to reawaken at 4:30 for the day, getting only four hours of sleep or less per night. This was a symptom of severe clinical depression. I prayed nonstop when I awoke. I prayed at work. I prayed on the way home from work.

I began to feel rage toward the man who was encouraging inappropriate behavior in me. I began to fantasize that I would ram into his car with mine whenever I saw it. Where were these thoughts coming from? I began feeling rage because I was responding seductively. I would say "no" to him mentally twenty or more times a day, promising myself I would not engage in the "turn-on/come on" behavior. Then whenever I saw him, my resistance would crumble and I would find myself doing exactly what I had vowed not to do. This caused me some very strong internal conflicts. I lived in a state of intense anxiety over trying to identify what was "right" or "wrong" behavior. There were so many worldly standards to choose from, yet none of them seemed capable of resolving my conflict once and for all. An excerpt from my journal at the time expresses the conflict and confusion I was experiencing:

Fidelity and righteousness—why can't I make up my mind? Is this behavior wrong or isn't it? Is it this hard for everyone to be "good"? What is my standard? What is God's standard? What is so difficult about this decision? Why do I have to make it daily and even more often? Why do my sisters know right from wrong and I don't? Why does certainty always seem to elude me on this question?

Interrupting the Cycle

I began to pray for fidelity and righteousness. Then, one day while I was riding my bicycle, my thoughts turned to this other man again in a powerful fantasy. Only this time the thoughts were interrupted by a powerful thought that literally blasted through my mind: "Be righteous for the sake of God!" I interpreted the thought in this way: I was to set right my behavior. I was to pursue rectitude of conduct. Out of consideration and regard for God I was to be righteous; meaning without guilt, fault, or blame. Not for myself, nor for my husband; but for God! The concept of obedience to authority crystallized in my mind. It was a powerful revelation. Righteousness—the word itself had healing power. I grabbed it like a raft in a whirlpool, not knowing whether there was any way out of the whirlpool.

For six months I was in agonizing conflict while I clung in prayer to the concept of righteousness. I was consumed by the need to find an answer to my conflict. I wanted to have no doubt about what behavior was correct. I didn't want to even think inappropriately. (I would later discover that this was impossible.) And at the end of six months, something happened that made me wonder if God had answered my prayers: A Bahá'í reentered my life.

A New Relationship

Because of the ongoing relationship with my new Bahá'í friend, I was encouraged to reconnect with Bahá'u'lláh and searched a copy of *Gleanings from the Writings of Bahá'u'lláh* for the one verse that had for some reason remained in my memory for ten years. I opened the book at the beginning and went through it page by page, scanning hopefully. I found the verse I was looking for: "Say: set ye aside My love, and commit what grieveth Mine Heart?"[1] I began to cry. I was grieving him by my behavior? It was such a compelling reproach.

The whole passage was exactly what I so desperately needed to read. It not only convinced me that my inclinations were corrupt and I needed to make the right choices, trusting that things would turn out right, but it also convinced me that this compelling, powerful Voice was the direction to which I should ever turn. The following extract captures the essence of the passage that spoke so directly to me:

> . . . Say: set ye aside My love, and commit what grieveth Mine heart? What is it that hindereth you from comprehending what hath been revealed unto you by Him Who is the All-Knowing, the All-Wise? We verily behold your actions. If We perceive from them the sweet smelling savor of purity and holiness, We will most certainly bless you. Then will the tongues of the inmates of Paradise utter your praise and magnify your names amidst them who have drawn nigh unto God.
>
> Cling thou to the hem of the Robe of God, and take thou firm hold on His Cord, a Cord which none can sever. Beware that the clamor of them that have repudiated this Most Great Announcement shall not deter thee from achieving thy purpose. Proclaim what hath been prescribed unto thee in this Tablet, though all the peoples arise and oppose thee. Thy Lord is, verily, the All-Compelling, the Unfailing Protector.[2]

I had an astounding revelation at this time: I realized that I had permission to tell this man "no." I had Bahá'u'lláh's permission. I remembered also that I was to seek "righteousness for the sake of God." I formally joined the Bahá'í Faith again in 1983, knowing deep in my soul that the power to heal lay in Bahá'u'lláh's revelation.

The mere act of declaring my belief in Bahá'u'lláh and becoming a Bahá'í was frightening to me. I knew I would have to face my husband, for he was and still is a deeply spiritual Christian. When I told John what I had done, he wept uncontrollably out of concern that I would be separating myself from Christ. I started to waver, but I held firm because I knew that the spiritual nourishment I had found in Bahá'u'lláh's writings would help me to heal from my illness. However, I must add that simply declaring my belief did not bring immediate healing and resolution to my dilemma with sexual acting out.

I began to understand that my anxiety attacks were connected to disobedience to God. "And if he feareth not God, God will make him to fear all things; whereas all things fear him who feareth God."[3] I had been telling the man "no" in my mind, but I had not actually done so outwardly. The hardest word for me to say out loud was "no." My weakest power for setting firm boundaries with others was the power of speech. I felt that Bahá'u'lláh was not only encouraging me to turn to a healing professional, but also urging me to learn obedience to the law of chastity. I was to discover that the "fear of God" was both a bounty and a power.

I had learned an outward, perfunctory "survival obedience" to avoid harsh punishment in my family of origin, but I had rebelled inwardly against true obedience. For someone like me, who had been severely traumatized by abuse, obedience to the truth of Bahá'u'lláh's revelation would have to come in stages. The stages of obedience can be likened to stages of perfection. First came the lessons; then came expanded consciousness, new perceptions, and a period of putting what I had learned into practice; then came obedience in response to the new perceptions, with further lessons and tests to follow.

I knew that acting out sexually was immoral, but my entire consciousness needed to be retrained. The major focus of my life from my earliest days had been sex. My first memories were of sex. During my developmental years I had been robbed of my chastity. On the subject of chastity Bahá'u'lláh says,

Purity and chastity . . . have been, and still are, the most great ornaments for the handmaidens of God. God is My Witness! The brightness of the light of chastity sheddeth its illumination upon the worlds of the spirit, and its fragrance is wafted even unto the Most Exalted Paradise.[4]

These words of Bahá'u'lláh would eventually become my standard, my anchor, my guide when doubts assailed me and temptations threatened my stability. But the change that was needed—the retraining and reorientation of my consciousness—did not happen overnight, and temptation still threatened my stability daily for quite some time.

Faith and Therapy Open the Doors

Around this time a long-standing physical problem forced me to have a series of tests done at the Mayo Clinic in Minnesota. I was born with two extra bones in my neck. They are called cervical ribs. A doctor in Rockford thought that if they were removed, I would be relieved of the physical stress they caused. The doctors at the Mayo Clinic decided that surgery would leave me with too much scar tissue, which could cause even greater pain. During the process of examination, however, the doctors asked me a strange question. They asked if I had been sexually abused. I said no; I was still keeping the secret, still trying to get on with my life, still trying to be loyal to my family, still trying to protect my father. The doctors ordered psychological tests, which indicated that I had indeed been sexually abused and needed treatment.

Apparently the clue that led the doctors to order the psychological tests was that I kept saying over and over again, in reference to my music, that I couldn't sing because my "instrument" was "damaged." Apparently, this is language a male would use to indicate that he has been sexually abused, the instrument being his penis. Why I, a female, was using such terminology, I do not know. But I had been found out, and I could no longer deny that I had a problem. Yes, I needed to explore with a therapist the burdensome secret that I had been carrying for almost forty-five years. I came back home to Rockford and sought psychological treatment.

In 1985, after reading Claudia Black's *Adult Children of Alcoholics,* I became aware that I was an adult child of an alcoholic, and I began studying codependency issues. My father, three of his brothers, my paternal grandfather, and other family members had suffered from alcoholism. I began attending Al-Anon meetings to see how this fit into my illness. It was extremely helpful to know that the first step of the twelve-step program was to admit your powerlessness. I certainly felt powerless about my sexual behavior.

In 1986 I heard of a twelve-step program for survivors of incest and sexual abuse. That is where I found the blessed release of speaking the forbidden secret out loud hundreds of times over a period of four years. After one year in the support group for survivors of incest, I was feeling very brave. I was telling the secret! However, I was deluded in thinking that the secret was really "out," because I had never discussed it with any of the principal characters of this drama—neither my father, nor my mother, nor my sisters.

Perhaps it sounds strange to say I was telling the secret aloud without *really* telling the secret. That's the power of the secret. The survivor of incest knows without ever being told that it is forbidden to talk about it. My father had died in 1972, and though I had never confronted him before his passing, during the Cuban Missile Crisis when all military forces were on alert, I had written a letter to him forgiving him for everything he had done when I was a child.

After his death my mother was going through his personal belong-
ings and found the letter, creased, tattered, and torn in his wallet.
In some small way I had communicated to him a willingness to
forgive. That he had preserved the letter for ten years communicated something meaningful to me, but the fact remained that I
had never confronted him and had never discussed the secret with
any member of my family.

It is not surprising that survivors of childhood sexual abuse do
not want to reveal or discuss the depravity in their families. It is not
pretty, and it is not a topic for polite conversation. But, apart from
the tiresome sensationalism created by the topic of incest as it is
exploited on daytime talk shows, one of the priceless benefits of
revealing the secret is that it enables those who have been traumatized to begin the process of healing.

It is important to note that every aspect of keeping the secret has
to be consciously united with the tools of human intelligence and
personality so that the person can achieve his or her true identity. Yet
the ability to do this is discounted by a perpetrator of abuse and by a
society that for centuries has protected the perpetrator, because our
culture and others are based on the doctrine of original sin.

I did not feel that I had permission to use these tools. The survivor uses every bit of being to keep the secret, so the focus of his or
her personality is skewed. We were created with many gifts within
us. All of our abilities were meant to help us mine those gifts. Yet if
our focus is to keep the secret, then we cannot develop our true
identity, which connects us with our internal intention, our true
purpose. If keeping the secret has become our singular obsession,
then the goal of therapy has to be to free the mind to achieve our
true purpose and enable the identity, the seat of our gifts, to develop. If we have been taught to obey authority blindly, we must
first feel that we have been granted permission to use all of our

human abilities and tools of intellect. I was to find that permission within Bahá'u'lláh's revelation.

Telling the Secret

I had been taught to blindly obey an unwritten law that says talking about the subject of my childhood sexual abuse within the family is forever forbidden. Mine was a whispered rebellion fomented behind the door of my support group, where there was no risk of upsetting my mother, my sisters, or my aunts and uncles on both sides of the family. The thing about an obsessive secret, once you start telling it in secret, is that you feel as though you will explode if you keep it inside. Now you have another secret: You're telling the secret. And when you start telling it, even in a whisper, you begin to want to tell everyone you meet. The pendulum swings from absolute silence to the desire to shout it from the rooftop. You feel out of control. And the more you tell it, the greater your anxiety because you could tell the wrong person, the forbidden person. The survivor would equate that with the realization of his or her deepest fear—ostracism from the family or the destruction of the family—and the horrible nightmare of the child could come true. It had never occurred to me that telling the secret to the forbidden person would be one of the keys to healing.

One day I was talking to my younger sister, and I accidentally said something in passing about "what Dad did to me." I had not intended to do it. It just slipped out. A rush of adrenalin hit me as my sister grasped the content of my words and grabbed my shoulders, asking, "*What* did Dad do to you?" I was rendered speechless for a moment by the swiftness of her reaction. Then began the outpouring of two hearts and memories as we compared notes. Now I had another secret. I had broken the unwritten rules. And when you break the unwritten family rules, you lose control of the secret. I found that I could not control my sister (thank God!). My anxiety heightened. This happened in September of 1987.

A month later in October, when I returned home from a vacation in Door County, Wisconsin, I found in my mail a copy of a letter my sister had written to our mother. In this letter my sister poured out all of her pent-up anger and animosity about the sexual abuse our father had perpetrated on us, naming me and disclosing what I had told her privately.

The secret was out, totally, forever. It was the beginning of hope for me. Because my sister had taken that brave step, I was able for the first time in my life, at age forty-six, to tell my mother what had happened. I was terrified, but for the first time in my life I felt I had permission to use my power of speech to speak the truth about the sexual abuse. I used the language of a child as I stumbled over words and grasped for ways to express myself. My mother listened quietly, reflectively, as she took it all in. She was full of questions, too. Another sister called, and another. My aunt in California called; she admitted that she had known about the abuse but remained silent at the time. We all began trading memories and sharing whatever facts we remembered.

The secret was out in a big way. And my world had not fallen apart. I now felt I had permission to talk about the secret, and I couldn't stop talking. I began to write an account of my abuse, which became the foundation for my first book, *Assisting the Traumatized Soul.*

In retrospect, I can see that my mother faced a very difficult situation when I was being abused. I know now that she instinctively did her best to protect her children's future. I consider her courage, tenacity, and willingness to suffer for the sake of keeping the family together to be among the sources of my healing. Because my mother managed to keep our family together through all of its tragedies, I was eventually able to trace patterns of abuse through three generations and begin to make sense of our suffering.

I also credit my father for his honesty when my mother questioned him about the accusation my sister had made. His admission of guilt validated my perception that the abuse had actually occurred, and this was vitally necessary for my healing. Other survivors of childhood sexual abuse are not as fortunate. They doubt their own perceptions of what has happened to them, and, lacking any external validation of those perceptions, their recovery is hindered.

Unblocking the Power of Speech

Once the secret was really out, I could examine it fully. Because my power of speech was no longer blocked, other memories began to surface. Thoughts that were forbidden were now unhindered because of my mother's encouragement. My ability to discriminate between right and wrong behavior increased because family members affirmed that my father's behavior had been terribly wrong. My sense of boundaries grew and with it my ability to protect myself. My self-knowledge grew and expanded to include history that had been denied our family. We realized a greater unity than we had ever known. For the first time, we were pulling together as a family.

To understand the importance of this in the context of other survivors who shared their suffering with me in the support group, it must be known that some survivors do not have access to their memories for a long time. Their memory is using its power to keep the secret from them as well as from their family, everyone with whom they do not feel safe. Other survivors do not have access to their emotions. They fear that if they were to allow themselves to feel the full power of their emotions, they would lose control of them as well as the secret. And still others have been so abused that they express their speech, thoughts, and viewpoints only in indirect ways, especially when they are in great fear. No two survivors are going to experience the repression of their identity in the same way. I believe that is why there is no magical formula to heal survivors of childhood sexual abuse. However, something "magical" happens when they realize they have the freedom or permission to talk in safety about what actually happened to them.

Progress in Forming
My New Identity—Will and Obedience

Carrying the secret causes fragmentation and paralysis of personal power. My thoughts, feelings, perceptions, discernment, self-knowledge, reflections, identity, speech, sense of boundaries, imagination, questions, choices, memory, intuition, understanding, wisdom, and physical senses all had to be validated over and over again as I revealed my secret.

The true purpose of therapy for me, and for so many others who have been similarly traumatized, is to develop, reassemble, and free the personality and intellect. And the true task of those who want to be obedient to God is to consciously develop the control over will and personal abilities that will support that quest for obedience. 'Abdu'l-Bahá, the eldest son of Bahá'u'lláh and the appointed interpreter of his teachings, states,

It is certain that man's highest distinction is to be lowly before and obedient to his God; that his greatest glory, his most exalted rank and honor, depend on his close observance of the Divine commands and prohibitions. Religion is the light of the world, and the progress, achievement and happiness of man result from obedience to the laws set down in the holy Books.[5]

Overcoming Dissociation—Learning to Express My Feelings

In the process of getting therapy, keeping a journal, attending weekly support group meetings, and studying the Bahá'í writings, I told my secret hundreds of times. I uncovered unconscious, distorted beliefs about myself. I learned that, periodically, I would go into a trancelike state of dissociation. I became aware of so many things: a distorted thinking process that recurred from generation to generation in my family; decisions I had made as a child and continued to make as an adult that were no longer consistent with my changing belief system; my participation in and responsibility for others' seductive and inappropriate sexual behavior. I became aware that I was created noble, and I finally recognized God's law of chastity, which is a spiritual law that is designed to protect our psychological and spiritual well-being. For me, the law of chastity encompasses not only the regulation of sexuality within marriage, but also a regulation of sexual fantasies. Certainly all of us have sexual fantasies, but if they dominate our lives they can be harmful. Many men and women suffer from sexual addiction. To stop this destructive behavior they have to gain control of their sexual fantasies and eliminate the viewing of pornographic images.

Another important part of my healing was learning to express my rage and anger in appropriate ways. The need for this prompted me to study anger and personal boundaries for seven years. Through my studies I learned that I have spatial boundaries as well as physical, sexual, property, intellectual, emotional, energy, monetary, and other boundaries. I learned that I could exert authority over all of these personal boundaries. I began to specialize in writing and teaching about anger and boundaries in workshops, conferences, and at a community college. This did much for my self-esteem, as I began to realize that my gifts and experiences could be used to offer something valuable to others who were hurting.

Learning about Boundaries

I invented the "Boundary Sculpting Game," which includes psychodrama techniques and role-playing. I created a video called *Louis Timothy, The Giant, Invisible Turtle*. Louis Timothy had become a giant turtle because he was holding in his angry feelings, and he had become invisible because he was afraid to tell others what he needed and who he was. The story of Louis won an award in London, England, and the video is now being used by Family Violence Shelters across the United States, including Hull House in Chicago, founded by Jane Addams. With the help of Dr. Storkess and Squirrel, Louis learns to consult about his anger, set boundaries with others, and share his feelings in an appropriate way. There are nine songs in this mini-musical, which were scored by Daniel Wedemeyer, who also wrote half of the songs.

The more I reached out to help others with these tools, the more my ability to express myself developed, and the more I began to feel at ease as a performer. Today I can express my anger verbally, not two weeks or two hours after the fact, but at the moment that it comes up, though sometimes I feel a lot of anxiety and self-doubt when I express it. Also, I am ever watchful to be responsible with my anger and am acutely aware of the need to maintain silence when it is required.

I have also performed in two musical plays, singing and acting on stage. Performing felt wonderful, even though I had continuous anxiety attacks before, during, and for three months after the plays were presented. The first play was "Cabaret," in which I played the role of Fraulein Schneider. Her major song was "I Will Survive." Talk about an appropriate role for a survivor! The second play was "Anything Goes," in which I played the character of Mrs. Harcourt and stole one scene by improvising when I lost my hat and my wig was askew. The audience roared!

Learning to Say "No"

With an expanded consciousness, new perceptions, new knowledge, and conscious motives, my ability to make decisions was greatly strengthened. As a result, I was finally able to say "no" to the man with whom I thought I was "in love" without changing my mind again and again. I ordered my own thoughts and my behavior. I set boundaries. I knew what was expected of me; I had permission to use my own authority, and I chose to obey the commandments of God. I had tried positive thinking. I had tried exercise for the depression; I had tried medicine, yoga, progressive relaxation, vitamins, therapy, and finally obedience.

Because my emotions were stabilized, I was able to work on other aspects of recovery that led to further growth and more complete obedience to the laws of God. I was also able to identify my distorted thought patterns, which helped immensely in reducing my depression. My obsession with the secret also subsided, and my mind was now free to focus on expressing my creative gifts. Door after door opened for me.

I had been passive, compliant, blindly obeying the unwritten law to keep the secret that I thought was essential to self-preservation, stability of the family, and protection of the perpetrator, but it had not worked. Instead of protecting me and my family, this behavior had perpetuated a cycle of abuse. It had kept me trapped for many years in old, dysfunctional patterns of thoughts and behaviors. It wasn't until the secret was out that I could finally put the abuse behind me and begin to fully accept my new, healthy, spiritual identity.

Obedience

O SON OF MAN!
Wert thou to speed through the immensity of space and traverse the expanse of heaven, yet thou wouldst find no rest save in submission to Our command and humbleness before Our Face.[6]

God calls each of us to healing through obedience to his laws, which set boundaries and limitations for our behavior. But as I explained earlier, I needed to combine obedience with rational thought, discernment, and reflection. I have learned that acting in blind obedience does not release me from life's lessons and tests, but using my spiritual gifts and powers in obedience to God's commandments does. I have learned that having a healthy, trusting obedience to God, which involves thinking and making wise choices, is quite different from blindly abdicating the power of choice to a tyrannical authority. I have also learned that consistent obedience is the result of God's giving me several lessons that evoked a thousand new choices for which I am grateful and a thousand new perceptions that fill me with wonder. Suddenly I experienced that "I get it!" feeling—the sense that God was on my side and was helping me make new choices, not trying to punish me.

I have learned that there are stages of obedience that advance from imperfection towards perfection. Each stage must be judged according to its own merits, not as right or wrong, good or bad, but with three questions in mind: What has been learned up to that point? What has yet to be learned? What is still blocking understanding? This is so much healthier than the traditional all-or-nothing concept of "good and evil."

In 1993, when I was fifty-two years old, my terrifying recurring dream that someone was approaching my bed in the dark recurred, I believe, for the last time. Once again the terror began to build as a figure approached my bed in my dream. Once again my mouth was sealed tightly as the desperate guttural sounds created a disturbing level of consciousness within my sleep. Then, incredibly, I sat bolt upright in my sleep and screamed a piercing "Noooooooooooo!" It echoed through decades of silence, exploding through the lips of a child who had finally been empowered to put a word to her preverbal rage: "NO!"

My husband awoke and comforted me. The new ending to my dream changed me. In that moment I felt reborn. I had gained control over myself through obedience to the will of God. I realize now that I could not have achieved stability until I had fully surrendered to God and chosen obedience to the law of chastity. A tiny, undeveloped entity within me has been empowered, through my obedience, to say "no!" Once I knew the laws, accepted them consciously, put them into practice, and finally stopped changing my mind, I learned to submit in trust to the internal boundaries I was setting. I became consistent mentally and behaviorally in all circumstances. My new spiritual identity was coming together. I was able to integrate all the component parts of my identity: What I think, feel, believe, imagine, say, am, desire, and do are governed by my obedience to the will of God.

God has retrained His child. He took me from the developmental stage of a child to maturity and taught me how to live. God cared for me as He cares for all.

5

Breaking the Intergenerational Cycle of Abuse

In chapter 4 I spoke at length about many aspects of my own healing journey. I spoke of the amazing breakthrough that occurred when I finally began to tell my secret and learned that I was not to blame for all that had happened to me. I learned to speak, to use my own voice to protect myself from harm. I learned about my own spiritual powers, which had been latent within me all along, and I began to be able to use the Bahá'í Faith and its guidelines as a foundation for my new emerging identity. I learned that my own thoughts, feelings, and perceptions were valid and could be relied upon when making choices for myself and my new life. I learned to express my thoughts and feelings in appropriate ways. I learned how to say "no" and how to walk away from situations that might harm me.

Slowly but surely I forged a healthy new identity that allowed me to begin to abandon old thoughts and behavior patterns that had been shaped and formed according to someone else's agenda. Before, as a child, I had no choice but to be swept up into my father's own horrific nightmare of unresolved traumas based on his own terrible and unresolved childhood issues.

Continued vigilance about obedience to God's commandments reduced chaos in my life. Daily prayer, routine participation in Bahá'í community life, service to others, and my own artistic and creative endeavors gave my life a form and a meaning that began to feel congruent and safe.

I could see myself making progress in stages. I was moving forward step by step. As the process unfolded, my old view of myself as either "all good" or "all bad" gave way to a compassionate view of myself as an emerging soul—a soul on a valiant and successful healing journey.

Mental Illness

Throughout this book I have emphasized that my spiritual life provided the foundation for my healing journey. Nonetheless, there were unavoidable mental health issues that could only be adequately addressed by seeking the help of competent professionals. I resisted this help. I wanted to believe that prayer and my own dogged determination alone would be enough to heal me. I was wrong. I was aware of a passage of Bahá'í scripture in which Bahá'u'lláh instructs us to seek the help of competent physicians when we are ill. He writes, "Resort ye, in times of sickness, to competent physicians; We have not set aside the use of material means, rather have We confirmed it through this Pen, which God hath made to be the Dawning-place of His shining and glorious Cause."[1]

In the year 2000, the diagnosis of bipolar disorder was confirmed. Before I accepted this diagnosis I had spent a year seeking help from four different psychiatrists, one after another, each of whom had given me a different diagnosis and prescribed different medication. None of these diagnoses seemed to fit, and the medications not only didn't help but actually seemed to undermine the equilibrium I was trying so hard to maintain. As a result, I was quite skeptical when I received this fifth diagnosis. How could I be sure it was correct? I decided to seek help from a Bahá'í psychiatrist whose judgment I trusted. After telling him my story, he confirmed that, yes, the diagnosis of bipolar disorder certainly fit the symptoms I described. He said that there are many types of bipolar disorder, which is why it is not easy to diagnose. He said he would guess that the type of bipolar disorder I was suffering from was hypermanic, which was apparently manifesting itself in me as the inability to stop creating. This explained why I have always had so many people tell me that I am the most creative person they have ever met!

Today I maintain my mental health by taking my medication regularly and being ever watchful against the things that I know can trigger a manic or depressive phase in me. I know that I have to avoid caffeine because it is a stimulant, and I have to make sure I get plenty of rest after performing, which creates an emotional high for me. I also require at least nine hours of sleep per night. I have learned to ask to have my needs met, and I make my needs known to others as clearly as I can. I have also learned to ask for acknowledgment from my husband when I feel insecure.

Whenever I catch myself thinking, "Everything is fine! I don't need to be on medication anymore!" I just do a quick review of my ancient and previous history and remind myself of all the erratic behavior and sorrow that were caused by my mistrust of authentic authority and the fact that the bipolar disorder went undiagnosed until I was fifty-eight years old. The old adage "Know thyself" is relevant here, as is the following passage from the writings of Bahá'u'lláh: ". . . the first effulgence which hath dawned from the horizon of the Mother Book is that man should know his own self and recognize that which leadeth unto loftiness or lowliness, glory or abasement, wealth or poverty."[2] I have come to know myself, and I have come to understand that I was created noble by God; therefore I protect myself and my family from potential difficulties by staying on my medication.

Family Unity

My family is very important to me. Today I not only have healthy relationships with all the members of my immediate family but also with my family of origin. None of us are without our problems, but we have a flexibility that helps us maintain unity without conflict, isolation, or estrangement. And even if one of us loses our balance temporarily, I don't lose mine as a result of that imbalance anymore. I have an emotional stability that is in stark contrast to the instability I used to experience. I can make others laugh, and that brings me even more joy. Moreover, I have a loving husband who treats me as I deserve to be treated. He has been and continues to be a copartner in everything I have achieved, many times at great sacrifice. He thinks of my needs in a way that no other person has ever done, and I am very grateful to him for this.

Spiritual Discipline

I have learned that the discipline of daily spiritual practice is a fundamental key to my health and happiness. My thoughts are not always perfect, but prayer and reading from holy scriptures brings me back to correct my actions. A daily prayer life is the key ingredient that holds all of this together. Prayers for forgiveness, prayers for assistance and nearness to God, prayers for protection, and prayers for my family—all combine to keep me alert and attentive to actions I can take toward the greater good of humanity.

Bahá'u'lláh has clearly explained in his writings the requirements for spiritual growth. I summarize them here:

1. Daily prayer

2. Daily reading of the sacred scriptures every morning and evening with "reverence, attention and thought"[3]

3. Prayerful meditation on the teachings of the Bahá'í Faith and how they apply to my life

4. Trying every day to bring my actions into accordance with the standards of the Bahá'í Faith

5. Teaching others about God

6. Giving service to others

Following these steps nourishes and strengthens me spiritually, helping me to draw closer to God.

Social Life and Performing

I missed out on a lot of the history of the world because I isolated myself for so many years out of self-protection, so at times I feel very ignorant. Today, however, I challenge myself to choose activities that will help me emerge from my self-made "cave" and learn about others by participating in a group. Recently I joined a women's choir named "Womansong," which performs from the fall through the spring, singing joyful, positive, uplifting songs that inspire the soul.

I also teach a workshop called "Protective Behaviors for Children" as a service project. This has involved conducting staff training sessions in schools, orphanages, and Catholic service agencies, including thirty-five days of travel in Thailand. While in Thailand, I trained a young woman who is now presenting the material to children in Japan. I also present "The Boundary Sculpting Game," which is a workshop that helps youth and adults become more conscious of personal boundaries.

I am a storyteller and have written stories of "Women and Girls as Heroes," which I have performed all over the United States, Japan, and even in China. Challenging myself to create and educate is the secret of my success. All of the things that I create and all of the services I offer are inspired by the writings of Bahá'u'lláh, which I connect to the issues mankind faces today such as racism, sexism, and abuse. In this way I share and teach through performance what I have learned through personal experience and my study of Bahá'í scriptures.

A Parent's Acknowledgment of Abuse

All of my personal progress was wonderful, and I was very grateful for it. However, I realized at one point that I had forgotten one important thing. My daughter! As I mentioned in earlier chapters, my relationship with my eldest daughter was troubled from the start. When she was born, I was suffering from severe depression. All I wanted to do was sleep. I wasn't even feeding her properly. I fluctuated wildly from not feeding her at all to force-feeding her to make up for my neglect.

This pattern of behavior wasn't limited to food. I vacillated between periods of permissive neglect in all areas and cruel, forceful imposition of my will. It was only natural for me, given the role model of my father, an authoritarian patriarch, to assume the same role in relationship to my children. My oldest daughter was the main object of this dynamic. She was the scapegoat, the target, and therefore became the carrier of all the pain from both my past and my father's past.

My healing journey eventually brought me face-to-face with the horrifying realization that, although I had not sexually abused my daughter, I had treated her in the same authoritarian way my father had treated me. What does a mother do when confronted with the terrible truth that while she has been struggling to heal herself, her own daughter, the one for whom she would give her life, has been the recipient of the legacy of trauma? What does a mother do when her whole struggle has been to free herself from guilt and shame and she suddenly finds that she cannot escape her own responsibility for unwittingly perpetuating the cycle of abuse? Is more self-condemnation the answer?

One day while I was having a telephone conversation with my daughter, she was lashing out at me in the cruelest fashion. I could hear in her voice both my own voice and that of my father. She lashed out at me. She whipped me with words. She cut my heart out, and I was vulnerable to it. It took every ounce of courage for me to stay on the phone with her and hear her out. In a moment of intuition I knew that the only way to her heart was acknowledgment, so, bravely, and point by point, I acknowledged her pain and her perceptions. I did it without self-blame as a pure acknowledgment of the truth of her agony. With each acknowledgment I suggested a possible new direction in which she might go. After thirty minutes of inspired words flowing from my lips, my daughter asked in a small, childlike voice, "Could you put that in writing for me?"

Out of respect for my daughter's wish that the following acknowledgment not be made public, I rewrote it as it appears here. When parents really change, they observe such privacy boundaries that will maintain trust and healing.

Unless there is acknowledgement of abuse, whether it happened two years ago or twenty or more years ago, justice has not been served. Pain untended and unacknowledged is humanity ignored. We feel our pain or we numb it. We carry the painful events within our hearts even if we forbid our memory to pull them out for examination. Without acknowledgment, decades of pain will ache untended, decades of fragmented memories will remain unresolved.

But the painful events and the memories can be laid to rest within our memory if justice has been received through simple heartfelt acknowledgement and the challenge of healing work is met. If the perpetrator of abuse is incapable of acknowledging the pain, then society must acknowledge the pain. If society does not acknowledge the pain, then it is, indeed, a random universe with no hope of meaning. Then pain unacknowledged will continue to create immobilizing mental, emotional, and physical distress, and unconsciousness will continue to produce perpetrators. It is for this purpose that the following acknowledgement of abuse has been written:

Dear Daughter,

As your mother, sometimes conscious sometimes aware, sometimes blessing, sometimes cursing, sometimes loving sometimes hateful, sometimes noble, sometimes abased, I fully acknowledge my inhumanity to you and the pain it has caused both of us.

I acknowledge that I was such a controlling, authoritarian parent that there was no room for you to question, challenge or say "no" in our relationship and that this has created an oppressive family life, as well as robbed you of the power to tell others "no." It also caused you tremendous pain and terror, immobilizing you, causing you shame and leaving you with the inability to confront others with their abusive behavior. I encourage you to seek out democratic methods of conducting family life and rearing children.

I acknowledge that you grew up unprotected and unguided at a time when childhood should have had a role model that showed you nurturing, leadership, courage, cooperation, responsibility, and discernment.

I acknowledge that my verbal abuse of you so humiliated you and my manipulating praise of you so confused you that you thought approval and disapproval of your self were solely the right of others and not an internal self-governing, self-accounting process. I encourage you to learn ways to build your own self-esteem and to adopt a healthy spirituality that will help create a peaceful, empowered you.

I acknowledge that I expressed disapproval when you tried to share unpleasant feelings like anger and that this shamed you to the point that you still have difficulty sharing anger with authority figures. I encourage you to learn safe, appropriate ways of expressing your anger to me and others.

I acknowledge that you had to make yourself invisible in order to escape my abusive treatment, and this created the lingering perception that it is never safe for you to share feelings, ideas, and opinions with others. I encourage you to be bold in stating what you think and feel . . . to let your voice be heard and your needs be known.

I acknowledge that I so overwhelmed you with impossible demands for perfection that I planted the seed of uncooperativeness within you, which grew and flourished into open rebellion. I encourage you to learn more effective ways of working with others.

I acknowledge that I shamed you for your childlike imperfections so that in order to not experience shame as an adult, you feel you have to be perfect. I encourage you to be gentle with yourself and others.

I acknowledge that I neglected my responsibility to teach you accountability when your behavior affected others in an adverse way so that you now, as an adult, do not notice when your behavior hurts or inconveniences others. I now know that permissiveness is abusive also, and I encourage you to learn the benefits of freedom within limitations.

I acknowledge that I covertly shamed you into secrecy about my own trauma so that you could not feel comfortable in sharing openly your pain about it, but were forced to act out my family secrets in ways that hurt you and hurt others. I encourage you to speak the truth and break this old, destructive cycle. Don't take on my pain. Listen to your own internal alarm that warns you when you are about to violate your own personal code of conduct.

I acknowledge that I clung to you only when I was desperate, depressed, and confused, so that you learned that you would receive love and achieve closeness only if you were my caretaker. I encourage you to find a well-balanced way of giving and receiving love, and I assert that I am responsible for finding a way out of my down moods.

I acknowledge that by not asserting myself and because of authoritarian beliefs and values, I did not protect you from mental, emotional and physical harm. I encourage you to grieve this tremendous loss and to try to find a way of resolving the confused feelings you must have toward me because I betrayed the precious child that you were. And if you cannot resolve them, I encourage you to find a surrogate mother, father, or therapist who will nurture you now the way that I could not then.

I state all of this not as an atonement, for I can never atone for such a wrong. Not in guilt, though my newly-awakened healthy conscience not only condemns my actions toward you as inexcusable, but because it also helps me recognize, define, and condemn the immorality that was perpetrated against me in my childhood by still another conscienceless perpetrator. And not in shame because my shame has guided me to a more humane, fully conscious response to other human beings.

But I state it purely as an acknowledgement of your pain, your courage, your humanity, your creativity and, most importantly, because it is imperative that you go into the future as shame free, as guilt free, and as conscious as possible.

For if you can consciously identify and define abuse without rationalizing, denying, and minimizing what I did to you, you will be in an ideal position to love and protect the children of the future.

I cannot use the abuse perpetrated against me as an alibi. I am responsible for my hate, my choices, my actions, and the results. That you are doing healing work and learning to love yourself is a miracle for which I am thankful. That you are learning to love me is a Grace for which I am in awe.

After writing this letter my whole body shook, and while I knew that this was a healing moment for both me and my daughter, I knew I had to do something for myself—something that acknowledged me as a woman, as an individual. For was I not a separate human being with my own aspirations and not simply my daughter's mother? I needed the courage to step out from the pain of the past, the humiliation of the past, and once I did, the misperceptions of no one would ever cower me again as they had. I needed to stop being emotionally dependent upon others, especially my children. The following statement became an acknowledgment of myself, my possibilities, and my future path:

If a woman can pursue her good against all odds, under the harsh gaze of all those she loves, all those who love her, all those who don't care for her, even those who don't know her . . . giving them their right to judge her every moment, every memory, every mistake on the way . . . and still find a way to love herself, take responsibility for her growth, and continue pursuing her good and the greater good, she will find that her nobility is a light that radiates from within, not from without!

I have this, and I wish it for you!

6

Spiritual Aspects
of Suffering

It is significant that Bahá'u'lláh, the Prophet and Founder of the Bahá'í Faith, whom Bahá'ís understand to be the Messenger of God for today, states that he "consented to be bound with chains that mankind may be released from its bondage."[1] To begin to appreciate the significance of this statement, one has to realize that this was an act of complete and utter submission to the will of God. The mission to which Bahá'u'lláh devoted his entire life—as has always been the case for every Messenger of God—resulted in endless hardships for himself.

The hardships Bahá'u'lláh suffered included abuse, imprisonment, exile, the loss of all worldly possessions, the death of a son, the undermining of his health, and many other afflictions. No ordinary human being would willingly undergo such suffering. Yet Bahá'u'lláh endured all of this for the sake of revealing God's will for humanity today so that the character of humankind might be transformed and the moral and spiritual qualities that are latent in human nature might be developed in those who respond. While Bahá'u'lláh experienced trauma, sorrow, abasement, and manifold sufferings, he assured us that it was to secure the freedom, liberty, abiding joy, and prosperity of humanity.

Note that he did not assume the identity of a victim of abuse. There is a huge difference between being a powerless victim and being the target of someone's ignorance and perversity. The essence of how powerful we truly are as created in God's image is embedded in the following verse from a prayer by Bahá'u'lláh: "Glorified art Thou, O Lord my God! I yield Thee thanks for that Thou hast made me the target of divers tribulations and the mark of manifold trials, in order that Thy servants may be endued with new life and all Thy creatures may be quickened."[2] Bahá'u'lláh retained his power through obedience to God, and so can we. And we can, in our turn, be of assistance to others who are seeking to be quickened to a new life. Bahá'u'lláh set the example of being patient throughout various tribulations and manifold trials.

Very few of us have a life that resembles a flourishing rose garden. Certainly none of us is free of suffering. At best, our lives are bittersweet simply because we count among our family and friends individuals who suffer daily sorrow and upheaval, or we ourselves may be dealing with unjustifiable suffering.

Tremendous comfort and assurance can be found in the writings of the Bahá'í Faith when we feel burdened with life's difficulties. There we learn that the sufferings, tests, and difficulties we encounter have meaning and purpose and actually bear hidden spiritual gifts. It is not always easy to see suffering from this paradoxical perspective, and sometimes it takes a very long time to reach such an understanding. But Bahá'u'lláh assures us that God "will never deal unjustly with any one, neither will He task a soul beyond its power."[3]

I have found the following selection of passages and prayers from Bahá'í texts particularly relevant and helpful when life's difficulties weigh on my heart.

The Hidden Benefits of Suffering

Men who suffer not, attain no perfection. The plant most pruned by the gardeners is that one which, when the summer comes, will have the most beautiful blossoms and the most abundant fruit.

The labourer cuts up the earth with his plough, and from that earth comes the rich and plentiful harvest. The more a man is chastened, the greater is the harvest of spiritual virtues shown forth by him. A soldier is no good General until he has been in the front of the fiercest battle and has received the deepest wounds.

—'Abdu'l-Bahá, *Paris Talks*, no. 14.7–10

The mind and spirit of man advance when he is tried by suffering. The more the ground is ploughed the better the seed will grow, the better the harvest will be. Just as the plough furrows the earth deeply, purifying it of weeds and thistles, so suffering and tribulation free man from the petty affairs of this worldly life until he arrives at a state of complete detachment. His attitude in this world will be that of divine happiness. Man is, so to speak, unripe: the heat of the fire of suffering will mature him. Look back to the times past and you will find that the greatest men have suffered most.

—'Abdu'l-Bahá, *Paris Talks*, no. 57.1

The Meaning of Tests and Suffering

To attain eternal happiness one must suffer. He who has reached the state of self-sacrifice has true joy. Temporal joy will vanish.

—'Abdu'l-Bahá, *Paris Talks*, no. 57.3

As to tests, these are inevitable. Hast thou not heard and read how there appeared trials from God in the days of Jesus, and thereafter, and how the winds of tests became severe? Even the glorious Peter was not relieved from the claws of trials. He wavered, then he repented and mourned the mourning of a bereaved one, and his lamentations reached the realms on high. Is it, then, possible to be saved from the trials of God? Nay, by the righteousness of the Lord! There is a great wisdom therein of which no one is aware save the wise and knowing.

Were it not for tests, pure gold could not be distinguished from the impure. Were it not for tests, the courageous could not be separated from the cowardly. Were it not for tests, the people of faithfulness could not be known from the disloyal. Were it not for tests, the intellectuals and the faculties of the scholars in great colleges would not develop. Were it not for tests, sparkling gems could not be known from worthless pebbles. Were it not for tests, nothing would progress in this contingent world. Were it not for tests, the Fishermen could not be distinguished from Annas and Caiaphas, who occupied positions of honor and value.

Were it not for tests, the face of Mary, the Magdalene, would not shed its light of steadfastness and certitude upon all horizons. These are some insights into the wisdom of tests which we have unfolded unto thee that thou mayest become cognizant of the mysteries of God in every cycle. Verily, I pray God to illumine your face as pure gold in the fire of tests.

—'Abdu'l-Bahá, in *Divine Art of Living*, pp. 86–87

I ask of God that thou, His husbandman, shalt plough the hard and stony ground, and water it, and scatter seeds therein—for this will show how skillful is the farmer, while any man can sow and till where the ground is soft, and clear of brambles and thorns.

—'Abdu'l-Bahá, *Selections*, no. 196.4

To attain eternal happiness one must suffer. He who has reached the state of self-sacrifice has true joy. Temporal joy will vanish.

—'Abdu'l-Bahá, *Paris Talks*, no. 57.3

The souls who bear the tests of God become the manifestations of great bounties; for the divine trials cause some souls to become entirely lifeless, while they cause the holy souls to ascend to the highest degree of love and steadfastness. They cause progress, just as they cause retrogression.

— 'Abdu'l-Bahá, in *Divine Art of Living*, p. 88

The Fruits of Suffering

Sorrow not if, in these days and on this earthly plane, things contrary to your wishes have been ordained and manifested by God, for days of blissful joy, of heavenly delight, are assuredly in store for you. Worlds, holy and spiritually glorious, will be unveiled to your eyes. You are destined by Him, in this world and hereafter, to partake of their benefits, to share in their joys, and to obtain a portion of their sustaining grace. To each and every one of them you will, no doubt, attain.

— Bahá'u'lláh, *Gleanings,* p. 329

Do ye not look upon the beginning of the affairs; attach your hearts to the ends and results. The present period is like unto the sowing time. Undoubtedly, it is impregnated with perils and difficulties, but in the future many a harvest shall be gathered, and benefits and results will become apparent. When one considereth the issue and the end, exhaustless joy and happiness will dawn.

— 'Abdu'l-Bahá, in *Divine Art of Living*, p. 88

As to the subject of babes and children and weak ones who are afflicted by the hands of the oppressors . . . for those souls there is a recompense in another world . . . that suffering is the greatest mercy of God. Verily that mercy of the Lord is far better than all the comfort of this world and the growth and development appertaining to this place of mortality.

—'Abdu'l-Bahá, quoted in J. E. Esslemont, *Bahá'u'lláh and the New Era*, p. 96

Learning to Accept Tests

Be generous in prosperity, and thankful in adversity.

—Bahá'u'lláh, *Epistle to the Son of the Wolf*, p. 93

When calamity striketh, be ye patient and composed. However afflictive your sufferings may be, stay ye undisturbed, and with perfect confidence in the abounding grace of God, brave ye the tempest of tribulations and fiery ordeals.

—'Abdu'l-Bahá, *Selections from the Writings of 'Abdu'l-Bahá*, no. 35.12

Be not grieved if thy circumstances become exacting, and problems press upon thee from all sides. Verily, thy Lord changeth grief into joy, hardship into comfort, and affliction into absolute ease.

—'Abdu'l-Bahá, in *Divine Art of Living*, p. 90

O God! Recompense those who endure patiently in Thy days and strengthen their hearts to walk undeviatingly in the path of Truth.

Grant then, O Lord, such goodly gifts as would enable them to gain admittance into Thy blissful Paradise.

—The Báb, *Selections from the Writings of the Báb*, p. 211

Prayers for Healing, Assistance, and Protection

Thy name is my healing, O my God, and remembrance of Thee is my remedy. Nearness to Thee is my hope, and love for Thee is my companion. Thy mercy to me is my healing and my succor in both this world and the world to come. Thou, verily, art the All-Bountiful, the All-Knowing, the All-Wise.

—Bahá'u'lláh, in *Bahá'í Prayers*, p. 96

Create in me a pure heart, O my God, and renew a tranquil conscience within me, O my Hope! Through the spirit of power confirm Thou me in Thy Cause, O my Best-Beloved, and by the light of Thy glory reveal unto me Thy path, O Thou the Goal of my desire! Through the power of Thy transcendent might lift me up unto the heaven of Thy holiness, O Source of my being, and by the breezes of Thine eternity gladden me, O Thou Who art my God! Let Thine everlasting melodies breathe tranquillity on me, O my Companion, and let the riches of Thine ancient countenance deliver me from all except Thee, O my Master, and let the tidings of the revelation of Thine incorruptible Essence bring me joy, O Thou Who art the most manifest of the manifest and the most hidden of the hidden!

—Bahá'u'lláh, in *Bahá'í Prayers*, pp. 164–65

Is there any Remover of difficulties save God? Say: Praised be God! He is God! All are His servants and all abide by His bidding!

—The Báb, *Selections,* p. 215

I adjure Thee by Thy might, O my God! Let no harm beset me in times of tests, and in moments of heedlessness guide my steps aright through Thine inspiration. Thou art God, potent art Thou to do what Thou desirest. No one can withstand Thy Will or thwart Thy Purpose.

—The Báb, *Selections,* p. 209

Ordain for me, O my Lord, and for those who believe in Thee that which is deemed best for us in Thine estimation, as set forth in the Mother Book, for within the grasp of Thy hand Thou holdest the determined measures of all things.

Thy goodly gifts are unceasingly showered upon such as cherish Thy love, and the wondrous tokens of Thy heavenly bounties are amply bestowed on those who recognize Thy divine Unity. We commit unto Thy care whatsoever Thou hast destined for us, and implore Thee to grant us all the good that Thy knowledge embraceth.

Protect me, O my Lord, from every evil that Thine omniscience perceiveth, inasmuch as there is no power nor strength but in Thee, no triumph is forthcoming save from Thy presence, and it is Thine alone to command. Whatever God hath willed hath been, and that which He hath not willed shall not be.

There is no power nor strength except in God, the Most Exalted, the Most Mighty.

—The Báb, in *Bahá'í Prayers,* pp. 149–50

He is God! O God, my God! Bestow upon me a pure heart, like unto a pearl.

—'Abdu'l-Bahá, in *Bahá'í Prayers,* p. 29

O God, guide me, protect me, make of me a shining lamp and a brilliant star. Thou art the Mighty and the Powerful.

—'Abdu'l-Bahá, in *Bahá'í Prayers,* p. 29

O God! Refresh and gladden my spirit. Purify my heart. Illumine my powers. I lay all my affairs in Thy hand. Thou art my Guide and my Refuge. I will no longer be sorrowful and grieved; I will be a happy and joyful being. O God! I will no longer be full of anxiety, nor will I let trouble harass me. I will not dwell on the unpleasant things of life.

O God! Thou art more friend to me than I am to myself. I dedicate myself to Thee, O Lord.

—'Abdu'l-Bahá, in *Bahá'í Prayers,* pp. 174–75

Lord! Pitiful are we, grant us Thy favor; poor, bestow upon us a share from the ocean of Thy wealth; needy, do Thou satisfy us; abased, give us Thy glory. The fowls of the air and the beasts of the field receive their meat each day from Thee, and all beings partake of Thy care and loving-kindness.

Deprive not this feeble one of Thy wondrous grace and vouchsafe by Thy might unto this helpless soul Thy bounty.

Give us our daily bread, and grant Thine increase in the necessities of life, that we may be dependent on none other but Thee, may commune wholly with Thee, may walk in Thy ways and declare Thy mysteries. Thou art the almighty and the Loving and the Provider of all mankind.

—'Abdu'l-Bahá, in *Bahá'í Prayers,* pp. 22–23

O my Lord! Thou knowest that the people are encircled with pain and calamities and are environed with hardships and trouble. Every trial doth attack man and every dire adversity doth assail him like unto the assault of a serpent. There is no shelter and asylum for him except under the wing of Thy protection, preservation, guard and custody.

O Thou the Merciful One! O my Lord! Make Thy protection my armor, Thy preservation my shield, humbleness before the door of Thy oneness my guard, and Thy custody and defense my fortress and my abode. Preserve me from the suggestions of self and desire, and guard me from every sickness, trial, difficulty and ordeal.

Verily, Thou art the Protector, the Guardian, the Preserver, the Sufficer, and verily, Thou art the Merciful of the Most Merciful.

—'Abdu'l-Bahá, in *Bahá'í Prayers*, p. 154

Never lose thy trust in God. Be thou ever hopeful, for the bounties of God never cease to flow upon man. If viewed from one perspective, they seem to decrease, but from another they are full and complete. Man is under all conditions immersed in a sea of God's blessings. Therefore, be thou not hopeless under any circumstances, but rather be firm in thy hope.

—'Abdu'l-Bahá, in *Selections from the Writings of 'Abdu'l-Bahá*, no. 178.1

7

Preventing and Treating Childhood Sexual Abuse

I sit with my two-and-a-half-year-old grandson on my lap, and waves of memories engulf me. I was once as trusting as he is. I was once as innocent, too. I think about the fact that my grandson has sexual boundaries and that others must protect them until he is old enough to learn how to protect them himself.

How sad that these are my first thoughts when I am with him, while other parents and grandparents delight in the pure joy of an emerging identity with all of its charm and beauty! However, it is precisely because other survivors of childhood sexual abuse and I have this sad awareness that the secret of sexual abuse is being exposed and, in some cases, prevented. The secret has always protected the perpetrator of abuse, who counts on this innocence, this lack of awareness, and lack of boundaries. For generations, mothers and fathers have cautioned their children to be wary of strangers. Survivors of sexual abuse know that it is the parent, the grandparent, the uncle, the aunt, the friend of the family, the neighbor, who is most likely to perpetrate such abuse.

I am fortunate to be aware of this fact, and so is my family. Many survivors are not aware of the need for sexual boundaries. I have taught my adult children protective behavior. It is their responsibility, in turn, to teach their children. To do otherwise would be irresponsible. For generations, ignorance of the problem has protected those who would act out their sickness under the cloak of darkness.

The statistics on childhood sexual abuse are staggering. Far from being the rare and unusual phenomenon that many people imagine it to be, childhood sexual abuse is an epidemic. Statistics given by the National Incident-Based Reporting System in a report released by the National Center for Juvenile Justice on the Sexual Assault of Young Children show that crimes against juvenile victims are the large majority of the sexual assaults handled by law enforcement agencies (67 percent). One of every seven victims was under the age of six, and over one-third of all sexual assaults involved a victim who was under the age of twelve.[1]

The statistics indicate that problems with sexual offending most often occur within the family setting. Nearly five of every six sexual assaults of young juveniles occurred in the family residence. Strangers were the offenders in just 3 percent of the sexual assaults against victims under age six, and 5 percent of the sexual assault victimizations of youth from ages six through eleven. What does this tell us? This tells us that childhood sexual abuse is occurring in our towns, our neighborhoods, among our children's classmates, among our children's friends.[2]

On any given day, approximately 234,000 offenders are convicted of rape or sexual assault under the care, custody, or control of corrections agencies. Nearly 60 percent of these offenders are under conditional supervision in the community.[3]

The Bahá'í Position against Childhood Sexual Abuse

The Bahá'í Faith has taken a firm, clear, and uncompromising position that the abuse of women and children or any other group is not to be tolerated. Fundamental to its most basic principles is the notion that all men, women, and children of all races, nations, religious, and cultural and socioeconomic groups, are equal. The principle of the oneness of humanity is the pivot around which all the other beliefs and teachings of the Faith revolve. Oneness is necessarily created by fair and just treatment of all. Oneness demands that no one person, group, or subgroup take upon themselves the power to control, subjugate, or oppress others. There is absolutely no justification and no moral or political grounds upon which such behaviors can be justified or tolerated.

In a letter written in January 1993 to an individual in response to questions about violence and sexual abuse of women and children, the Universal House of Justice (the international governing body of the Bahá'í Faith) condemns such behavior and exhorts Bahá'ís to make every effort possible to end these deplorable practices. The letter calls for a "fundamental change in the manner in which people relate to each other" and an end to practices "which deny the intrinsic human right of every individual to be treated with consideration and respect." "The use of force by the physically strong against the weak, as a means of imposing one's will and fulfilling one's desires, is a flagrant transgression of the Bahá'í Teachings," the letter says. "There can be no justification for anyone compelling another, through the use of force or through the threat of violence, to do that to which the other person is not inclined."[4]

Addressing the issue of childhood sexual abuse, the letter states,

It is difficult to imagine a more reprehensible perversion of human conduct than the sexual abuse of children, which finds its most debased form in incest. At a time in the fortunes of humanity when . . . "The perversion of human nature, the degradation of human conduct, the corruption and dissolution of human institutions, reveal themselves . . . in their worst and most revolting aspects," and when "the voice of human conscience is stilled," when "the sense of decency and shame is obscured," the Bahá'í institutions must be uncompromising and vigilant in their commitment to the protection of the children entrusted to their care, and must not allow either threats or appeals to expediency to divert them from their duty. A parent who is aware that the marriage partner is subjecting a child to such sexual abuse should not remain silent, but must take all necessary measures . . . to bring about an immediate cessation of such grossly immoral behaviour, and to promote healing and therapy."[5]

Parental Rights Can Be Removed

While the teachings of the Bahá'í Faith exalt the role of parenthood and enjoin children to honor and obey their parents under all circumstances, the Universal House of Justice says that childhood sexual abuse so flagrantly and maliciously violates the sacred character of the bond between parent and child as to potentially render it null and void. Their letter of January 1993 states, "Bahá'u'lláh has placed great emphasis on the duties of parents toward their children, and He has urged children to have gratitude in their hearts for their parents, whose good pleasure they should strive to win as a means of pleasing God Himself. However, He has indicated that under certain circumstances, the parents could be deprived of the right of parenthood as a consequence of their actions."[6]

The Need for Community Intervention

Given the widespread nature of childhood maltreatment, its insidious nature, and its tendency to hide behind a cloak of secrecy erroneously protected under the rubric of "the privacy of the family," it is incumbent upon all men and women of just mind and sound heart to take up the battle to protect children. Protecting the young people in our own families, communities, neighborhoods, and schools is not the job of professionals. There are not enough professionals to go around. The problem is too big, too widespread, too insidious and pernicious. It has been allowed to fester and spread because often those who have knowledge that a child is being harmed choose to do nothing to stop it. They may say things to themselves like "It is none of my business." "I can't be certain it is happening, I have no proof." "If I tell my (uncle, brother, mother, niece, etc.), he/she will never speak to me again." "I have to preserve peace in the family." "I don't want to get involved." There are many reasons to duck the responsibilities for protecting a child whom you may suspect is being harmed. None of them are valid. My own story is a case in point.

After I began telling the secret of my own abuse openly to the world, many relatives came forward and said that they knew that the abuse had been going on. Any one of them could have taken steps to stop the abuse. How is that done? By reporting it to the police or child welfare agencies that exist in every locality all over the United States.

How To Report Abuse

Throughout the United States, in every locality, child abuse is by law an offense that requires an immediate response from law enforcement and child protection agencies. Reports of suspected abuse can be made to these agencies anonymously. You do not have to get personally involved if you do not want to. If you do not know who to contact, phone the local police department and tell them. They will direct your call. Another option is to go to a local hospital or emergency room or to a local doctor. They will be able to tell you how to make the report and how to protect your own privacy and confidentiality. Doctors, nurses, and other health care professionals, including psychologists and social workers, are bound by law in most states to report any suspected child abuse. Stopping child abuse is your job, your neighbor's job—it is everybody's job. Just dial 911 and ask how to report child abuse. It is that easy to make a difference.

Don't Be Discouraged If Immediate Action Is Not Effective

Don't be discouraged if you report suspected child abuse and nothing seems to change immediately. Often perpetrators deny their abuse. Victims often fear being forthright, especially the first time they are confronted with an opportunity to divulge the secret. In the case of incest, children feel loyal to their parents and love their parents even when they are being abused. They also fear reprisals. They may fear that reporting or fully disclosing the abuse will increase its severity. They may even fear that if they tell you what is being done to them, the abuser will kill them. Or they may fear reprisals against their siblings. They may fear that their parent will go to jail. They may fear they will cause a divorce. All too often, abusers threaten such consequences to try to keep children from telling others about the abuse.

Nevertheless, reporting abuse is critically important because the state agencies that handle these cases keep records. Perhaps after the first report or even the second report the perpetrator may be able to avoid detection. But as time goes by and reports mount, the authorities will become more and more inclined to take effective action as evidence accumulates that the reports have validity.

Defining the Many Forms of Abuse

Abuse is defined as behavior of one person toward another that harms that person physically, psychologically, emotionally, or spiritually. Abuse is an attempt to oppress or gain power over another. Abusers put their own needs and wants above those they exploit and use their victims to get what they want, be it physical pleasure, domination and control, financial gain, or other personal desires.

It is important to realize that people who are being abused often tolerate the abuse because they do not have the means or the resources to extricate themselves from the abusive situation. Once abuse has begun, only the abuser can stop it. Victims of abuse cannot stop the abuse. They can only try to escape from it, and in the case of children such escape is almost always impossible without the assistance of an adult.

Types of Child Abuse

The following list includes some of the types of child abuse that can occur. This list is by no means complete, and many types of abuse can occur concurrently.

Physical abuse includes the striking, slapping, or hitting of a child on any part of the body, which results in bruises, welts, scratches, or broken bones. Sometimes the injuries are of such severity that there is internal hemorrhaging. The causes of physical abuse can range from parental ignorance of healthy, nonviolent ways of disciplining children to battering the child while in a drunken rage or under the influence of drugs.

Physical neglect includes deprivation of food, clothing, shelter, or medical treatment.

Emotional neglect and *mental abuse* occur when caregivers do not show an interest in the child and reject or verbally humiliate him or her. The child may be denied emotional responsiveness to his or her needs or deprived of the encouragement necessary for the development of his or her self. Leaving a child at home alone is a potentially dangerous form of neglect. Terrorizing or frightening a child into obedience is considered mental abuse, as is living with the possibility that a sibling or parent could be physically battered at any moment.

When children experience such emotional and mental abuse, it causes severe emotional and mental distress and disempowers them at a time when their self-esteem and identity are being formed. Furthermore, neglect and actual abandonment will traumatize a child.

Sexual abuse is the coercion of a person—a victim—into meeting the sexual demands of another person, the perpetrator. This kind of abuse can damage one's self-esteem, one's relationships with others, one's sexual development, one's trust in others, and one's ability to achieve success. Such abuse is often associated with disorders such as overeating, bulimia, anorexia, and various forms of chemical dependence. Sadly, it is not uncommon for children who are abused in other ways—and are thus starving for affection and attention—to be abused sexually, because they are easily coerced into meeting the demands of the perpetrator, who plays on their trust and vulnerability.

Incest is sexual abuse inflicted upon a child by a parent or other close relative. It can be broadly defined to include anything from inappropriate sexual innuendo, to forcing a child to look at pornography, to actual intercourse, sodomy, or other forms of sexual activity.

Emotional incest is difficult to define because it can be far more subtle. For example, parents who openly talk about specific sexual acts in front of their children create an atmosphere of emotional incest. Chronic nudity or nudity at inappropriate times is also abusive. Children who are forced to listen to or watch caretakers or other adults engaging in sexual activity with each other are being abused. Hearing adults call each other sexual names is also traumatizing, as is living with the daily threat of personal sexual abuse when observing the sexual abuse of a sibling.

Spiritual Abuse

There is yet another type of abuse that should be mentioned here: spiritual abuse. Spiritual abuse is oppression of the soul—whether by religious authority, parental authority, or institutional authority—that distorts truth and spiritual teachings and thereby interferes with the victim's ability to develop spiritually. This kind of abuse can corrupt or pervert the character of the victimized man, woman, or child as it is developing. The victim of such abuse does not know where to turn for mercy and guidance and may be unable to discern good moral choices. Bahá'u'lláh refers to this type of

abuse as "oppression." He writes, "What 'oppression' is more grievous than that a soul seeking the truth, and wishing to attain unto
the knowledge of God, should know not where to go for it and
from whom to seek it?" He explains, ". . . by oppression is meant
the want of capacity to acquire spiritual knowledge and apprehend
the Word of God."[7]

Children Tend to Blame Themselves

Whatever the type of abusive treatment and whatever the circumstances, the child who is abused usually internalizes a distorted
belief system that is based on the idea that he or she is worthless,
guilty, and blameworthy. If victims of sexual abuse interpret their
own participation in the abuse as having been willing, or if they
have experienced pleasure while being sexually abused, they may
blame themselves instead of the perpetrator. "If only I hadn't seduced him." "If only I hadn't worn shorts to the picnic." "It was my
fault because I got in bed with her." This type of thought process
has to be revealed for what it is: absolution of the responsibility of
the perpetrator of abuse.

Part of the healing journey for victims of childhood sexual abuse
requires that they realize they are not to blame and that their childhood experiences have affected their brain and nervous system and
changed their perceptions and thought processes. Healing is sometimes a slow process because old nervous system patterns established during episodes of abuse and old ways of coping with the
abuse have to be "unlearned." New, adaptive patterns must be learned
and literally "absorbed" into the nervous system in the form of new
nervous system patterns.

Unlearning is always more difficult than learning, but learning new material is made more difficult when old, maladaptive material must first be "unlearned." That is one reason why the healing journey from child abuse can take a long time. It is also a reason to report abuse as soon as you suspect it. The earlier child abuse is stopped, the more positive the prognosis for the victim. The reason for this is that young children have nervous systems that are very amenable to change. If they are hurt, they can heal more quickly than adults can when the abusive behavior is stopped and they are made to feel safe and given the opportunity to heal. This is why it is crucial that the abuse be stopped immediately. Waiting until the child is an adult to report abuse or thinking that the child can "deal with it" better after he or she reaches a more mature age is absolutely false! A child needs immediate protection from abuse, and this immediate action greatly increases the chance that healing will be fast and comprehensive.

Some of the Myths Surrounding Child Abuse

There are many myths surrounding the issues of childhood sexual abuse. These myths distort the truth about abuse and contribute to the low incidence of reporting abuse to authorities. I will list some of these myths here and discuss them briefly.

Myth: Children "want" to be sexually abused.
Answer: This is completely untrue. This is an argument that abusers have often used to defend their behavior in an effort to absolve themselves of responsibility for what they have done. By

blaming the child for the behavior, they believe that they can abdicate their own moral culpability.

Myth: Children seduce adults.
Answer: This, too, is false. Adults have more power than children. An adult who does not want to engage a child in sexual activity has the power to stop it. The adult in such a scenario is responsible, not the child. Furthermore, for the most part, children do not spontaneously become sexually active until around the time of puberty unless they are exposed to sexual material earlier. Very, very young children do not know anything about adult sexuality. If you see very young children acting out adult sexual behavior either with other children or with dolls, or in other ways, immediately investigate the origins of this behavior. Ask the child where they learned about this type of "play." It is possible that someone is teaching the child about this type of activity. It is your job to find out where they are learning about this kind of behavior.

Myth: If children are exposed to explicit sexual material in magazines, books, videos, television, or movies it will not harm them.
Answer: This, too, is false. Premature exposure to explicit sexual material can have an effect on children that is very harmful. Children should not be exposed to any sexual content. If they are exposed to these materials, steps should be taken to help them understand the experience and put it behind them.

Myth: You should never talk to children about sex.
Answer: This is false. If a child brings up questions related to sex, his or her questions should be answered in terms that he or she

can understand, without giving more information than the child is ready to handle. Our culture barrages children with sexual content in the media at an alarming rate and with such frequency that most children become exposed to issues like homosexuality, infidelity, and other issues at a very young age. If they have questions about such matters, answer the questions in the context of a discussion of moral, upright behavior that you recommend. Don't be afraid to tell your children that some people use sex in ways that you do not believe are good for them. Keep it simple, but be straightforward. Opening the dialogue around these difficult issues can be a way to prevent your child from becoming trapped in an abusive situation that they feel they cannot discuss with anyone.

Myth: Sex between adults and children is good for the children. It educates them about sex and prepares them for life.
Answer: This is absolutely false. As amazing as it may sound to you, there are people who actually believe this. There are even organizations that support sexual activity between adults and children.

Myth: Sexual abuse of children does not happen within trusted community organizations or religious communities.
Answer: This is false. Abuse can occur anywhere and can even be perpetrated by individuals who are highly trusted and hold positions of authority. These statements are made not to condemn anyone, nor are they made to spread paranoia. Nevertheless, it is important that an attitude of prudent protection and moderate vigilance prevail when it comes to protecting children from exploitation.

Myth: If you suspect a child has been abused, it is better not to mention it to the child unless his or her behavior becomes very obvious and extreme.

Answer: This is false. If sexual abuse is suspected *at all* it is best to have a loving and supportive dialogue with the child. Make sure the person having this dialogue is comfortable with the conversation and proceeds in a low-key, kind, and inquisitive manner.

Myth: If suspected child abuse is reported to the authorities and no corrective action is taken, it can be correctly assumed that no abuse is taking place. It is best, therefore, never to mention the issue again.

Answer: This is false. It is best to have a discussion about the worrisome behavior and to keep the door open for further discussions in the future. It is especially important to continue to monitor the issue with a heightened level of care and greater attention to safety for the child.

A Personal Example

It is not always easy to do the right thing when it comes to reporting abuse. I will tell you a story from my own life to illustrate this point.

When my daughter was six years old she had a friend named Daniel, who was also six years old at the time. His mother was nine months pregnant. My daughter and Daniel went to school together. I was enrolled in a psychology course at Rock Valley College and doing very well. I was getting As and enjoying my classes as I had never enjoyed them before. However, for some reason I couldn't figure out at first, my daughter was going through some sort of terrible stress. She was experiencing diarrhea every day. She was losing weight. Every morning she would cry and say she didn't want to go to school. This confused me because I knew that previously she had loved school. I decided to go to school with her every day to see if I could understand why she was so ill. This would mean that I would have to sacrifice my class. The feeling deep in my heart was that it was necessary.

As I sat in the back of the classroom observing, I heard yelling and screaming. The teacher across the hall was screaming as she was hitting someone over and over. I was shocked because I knew it was Daniel. My daughter, who loved Daniel, was too young to verbalize the injustice he was enduring. She was witnessing Daniel's being beaten every day. I went to school every day to support my daughter and Daniel. I prayed each day that I could find a resolution to the problem. I didn't know what the school's policy about corporal punishment was. I just knew the situation was wrong and that I needed to be a compassionate observer so I would know how to proceed. Daniel needed protection. His mother could not handle the problem at her stage of pregnancy. So finally, though I was fearful of authority, I went into action, bringing documentation of my week in class to the attention of the appropriate authority.

Shaking in my shoes, I reported the incidents that I had observed to the principal. The abusive teacher was fired. My daughter was relieved of her anxiety. Even though I had fallen so far behind in my psychology class that I had to withdraw, I felt it was worth it. I had done the right thing by sacrificing my own needs to put the needs of my daughter first. I had taken difficult steps to serve as an advocate for a child, Daniel, who had no other advocate. Later on, I went on to study psychology independently and lost nothing in my schooling because of my sacrifice.

A Note of Caution about Friendships between Adults and Children

Adults who seduce children into sexual activity with them often do so after a period of what is called "grooming." "Grooming" is a manipulative plan in which a child abuser makes friends with a child and with the child's parents or guardians. During the grooming period the soon-to-be abuser is kind and supportive toward the child and engenders the parents' trust. Once trust is established and as the potential abuser is able to spend more and more time alone with the child, the stage is set for abusive sexual activity to be gradually introduced under a variety of guises. Abusers will often tell the child that the activity is "normal" or "a game" or "fun and exciting." Sometimes pornography is introduced to open the door to inappropriate sexual activity.

Those who work with sexually abusing adults and those who work in child protection agencies advise parents to be wary of adults who want to spend periods of time alone with their children. Particular caution should be exercised regarding any "sleepovers" or periods of travel away from home when the child could be put in compromising situations and would not have access to help from parents and family members should problems arise.

The Role of Friends, Family, and Community

What is our role as friends or family members who love and care for one another? If children are being abused in the home, then we need to seek justice for those children. We need to press compassionately for intervention. Justice will be served not by judging and condemning, but by seeking out a competent professional who knows how to work out abuse issues and work through traumatic memories.

Those who have been traumatized need to be empowered, and they need hope. The revelation of Bahá'u'lláh can provide both. Those who have been traumatized need to grieve for what has been lost to them in order to resolve the trauma. Friends and trained professionals can take them through the natural sequence of grieving: denial, sadness, anger, and acceptance. Committed friends can let them know that someone is open to hearing about their anger and sadness. Such friends need to listen without judging, letting the victim of abuse know that there are places to get help, and acting as their advocate if they suffer from a sense of helplessness that seems to debilitate them. Friends can help the traumatized understand that authority can be merciful and just and can direct them toward professional help if it is needed. They can encourage responsible behavior that will help to improve their self-esteem.

When Is Professional Intervention Needed?

When a child is discovered to have been sexually abused, professional help is needed to help the child and family heal. The treatment time may be short or prolonged, depending on the nature of the events. However, it is extremely important that the event not be simply "swept under the rug." Long-term healing is best achieved when prompt, supportive, appropriate measures are taken as soon as possible after the abusive events occurred.

Adult survivors of childhood sexual abuse need professional help when the symptoms of abuse interfere with their ability to function effectively. For example, repeated or frequent flashbacks, anxiety attacks, and panic attacks related to the abuse, or an inability to perform well on the job because of a feeling of being "spacey" (going in and out of a trance) would suggest that help is needed. Other indicators that intervention is necessary are the revealing of relationship problems related to children or spouse, sexual problems, suicide attempts, or the abuse of children at home. Substance abuse, addictions to work, eating disorders, and other symptoms may accompany a history of abuse.

The Result of Abuse: The Deprivation of Power

The end result of all physical, sexual, spiritual, emotional, and mental abuse is that it disempowers the victim. Any kind of tyrannical or oppressive behavior disempowers. In society, tyranny can be defined as any arbitrary use of authority that is unchecked by legitimate laws or constitutional limits. In society, victims of tyranny, authoritarianism, or oppression are not allowed to receive their due rights within the social contract, and in the process of using their energy to develop mechanisms of defense to cope with this abuse, they lose the power to develop fully and exercise appropriately the capacities that would allow them to become mature, contributing members of society in the future.

Further Reading

For those who wish to delve a little deeper than this brief summary of abuse, I suggest reading the following books, which have been extremely helpful to me: *Outgrowing the Pain,* by Eliana Gill; *Secret Survivors,* by E. Sue Blume; *The Courage to Heal,* by Ellen Bass and Laura Davis; and *Inside Scars,* by Sheila Sisk and Charlotte Foster Hoffman.

For an introduction to family dynamics, I found *The Family* and *Healing the Shame that Binds,* by John Bradshaw, very helpful.

To understand the roots of violence, you may wish to consider the following titles by Alice Miller, a Swiss psychoanalyst: *For Your Own Good* and *Thou Shalt Not Be Aware.* These are all classics in the field and have stood the test of time.

Newer books in the field include *Surviving Childhood Sexual Abuse,* by Carolyn Ainscough and Kay Toon; *Beginning to Heal,* by Ellen Bass and Laura Davis; *Understanding Child Abuse and Neglect,* by Cynthia Crosson-Tower; *Abused Boys,* by Mic Hunter; and *No Visible Wounds,* by Mary Susan Miller, Ph.D.

Three excellent books authored by Bahá'ís are *It's Not Your Fault: How Healing Relationships Change Your Brain & Can Help You Heal from a Painful Past,* by Patricia Romano McGraw, Ph.D.; *Overcoming Violence against Women and Girls: The International Campaign to Eradicate a Worldwide Problem,* by Michael Penn and Rahel Nardos; and *The Psychology of Sprituality: From Divided Self to Integrated Self,* by Hossain B. Danesh.

Appendix 1:

Violence and Sexual Abuse of Women and Children

A document prepared by the Department of the Secretariat of the Universal House of Justice,* 24 January 1993

Dear Bahá'í Friend,

Further to our letter of 14 November 1991, the Universal House of Justice has now completed its consideration of your letter of 21 September 1991, in which you raised a number of questions pertaining to violence and to the sexual abuse of women and children. We have been instructed to provide the following response to your questions.

As you know, the principle of the oneness of mankind is described in the Bahá'í Writings as the pivot round which all the Teachings of Bahá'u'lláh revolve. It has widespread implications which affect and remold all dimensions of human activity. It calls for a fundamental change in the manner in which people relate to each other, and the eradication of those age-old practices which deny the intrinsic human right of every individual to be treated with consideration and respect.

Within the family setting, the rights of all members must be respected. 'Abdu'l-Bahá has stated:

> The integrity of the family bond must be constantly considered and the rights of the individual members must not be transgressed. The rights of the son, the father, the mother—none of them must be transgressed, none of them must be arbitrary. Just as the son has certain obligations to his father, the father, likewise, has certain obligations to his son. The mother, the sister and other members of the household have their certain prerogatives. All these rights and prerogatives must be conserved. . . .

---

* The Universal House of Justice is the nine-member international governing council of the Bahá'í Faith.—Ed.

The use of force by the physically strong against the weak, as a means of imposing one's will and fulfilling one's desires, is a flagrant transgression of the Bahá'í Teachings. There can be no justification for anyone compelling another, through the use of force or through the threat of violence, to do that to which the other person is not inclined. 'Abdu'l-Bahá has written, "O ye lovers of God! In this, the cycle of Almighty God, violence and force, constraint and oppression, are one and all condemned." Let those who, driven by their passions or by their inability to exercise discipline in the control of their anger, might be tempted to inflict violence on another human being be mindful of the condemnation of such disgraceful behavior by the Revelation of Bahá'u'lláh.

Among the signs of moral downfall in the declining social order are the high incidence of violence within the family, the increase in degrading and cruel treatment of spouses and children, and the spread of sexual abuse. It is essential that the members of the community of the Greatest Name* take utmost care not to be drawn into acceptance of such practices because of their prevalence. They must be ever mindful of their obligation to exemplify a new way of life distinguished by its respect for the dignity and rights of all people, by its exalted moral tone, and by its freedom from oppression and from all forms of abuse.

Consultation has been ordained by Bahá'u'lláh as the means by which agreement is to be reached and a collective course of action defined. It is applicable to the marriage partners and within the family, and indeed, in all areas where believers participate in mutual decision making. It requires all participants to express their opinions with absolute freedom and without apprehension that they

* The Bahá'í community; "the Greatest Name" is an allusion to the name of Bahá'u'lláh, which means in Arabic "the Glory of God."—Ed.

will be censured or their views belittled; these prerequisites for success are unattainable if the fear of violence or abuse is present.

A number of your questions pertain to the treatment of women, and are best considered in light of the principle of the equality of the sexes which is set forth in the Bahá'í Teachings. This principle is far more than the enunciation of admirable ideals; it has profound implications in all aspects of human relations and must be an integral element of Bahá'í domestic and community life. The application of this principle gives rise to changes in habits and practices which have prevailed for many centuries. An example of this is found in the response provided on behalf of Shoghi Effendi* to a question whether the traditional practice whereby the man proposes marriage to the woman is altered by the Bahá'í Teachings to permit the woman to issue a marriage proposal to the man; the response is, "The Guardian wishes to state that there is absolute equality between the two, and that no distinction or preference is permitted. . . ." With the passage of time, during which Bahá'í men and women endeavor to apply more fully the principle of the equality of the sexes, will come a deeper understanding of the far-reaching ramifications of this vital principle. As 'Abdu'l-Bahá has stated, "Until the reality of equality between man and woman is fully established and attained, the highest social development of mankind is not possible."

The Universal House of Justice has in recent years urged that encouragement be given to Bahá'í women and girls to participate in greater measure in the social, spiritual and administrative activities of their communities, and has appealed to Bahá'í women to arise and demonstrate the importance of their role in all fields of service to the Faith.

---

* The title by which Shoghi Rabbání (1897–1957), the great-grandson of Bahá'u'lláh, is generally known to Bahá'ís. He was appointed Guardian of the Bahá'í Faith by 'Abdu'l-Bahá and assumed the office upon 'Abdu'l-Bahá's passing in 1921.—Ed.

For a man to use force to impose his will on a woman is a serious transgression of the Bahá'í Teachings. 'Abdu'l-Bahá has stated that:

> The world in the past has been ruled by force, and man has dominated over woman by reason of his more forceful and aggressive qualities both of body and mind. But the balance is already shifting; force is losing its dominance, and mental alertness, intuition, and the spiritual qualities of love and service, in which woman is strong, are gaining ascendancy.

Bahá'í men have the opportunity to demonstrate to the world around them a new approach to the relationship between the sexes, where aggression and the use of force are eliminated and replaced by cooperation and consultation. The Universal House of Justice has pointed out in response to questions addressed to it that, in a marriage relationship, neither husband nor wife should ever unjustly dominate the other, and that there are times when the husband and the wife should defer to the wishes of the other, if agreement cannot be reached through consultation; each couple should determine exactly under what circumstances such deference is to take place.

From the Pen of Bahá'u'lláh Himself has come the following statement on the subject of the treatment of women:

> The friends of God must be adorned with the ornament of justice, equity, kindness and love. As they do not allow themselves to be the object of cruelty and transgression, in like manner they should not allow such tyranny to visit the handmaidens of God. He, verily, speaketh the truth and commandeth that which benefiteth His servants and handmaidens. He is the Protector of all in this world and the next.

No Bahá'í husband should ever beat his wife, or subject her to any form of cruel treatment; to do so would be an unacceptable abuse of the marriage relationship and contrary to the Teachings of Bahá'u'lláh.

The lack of spiritual values in society leads to a debasement of the attitudes which should govern the relationship between the sexes, with women being treated as no more than objects for sexual gratification and being denied the respect and courtesy to which all human beings are entitled. Bahá'u'lláh has warned: "They that follow their lusts and corrupt inclinations, have erred and dissipated their efforts. They, indeed, are of the lost." Believers might well ponder the exalted standard of conduct to which they are encouraged to aspire in the statement of Bahá'u'lláh concerning His "true follower," that: "And if he met the fairest and most comely of women, he would not feel his heart seduced by the least shadow of desire for her beauty. Such an one, indeed, is the creation of spotless chastity. Thus instructeth you the Pen of the Ancient of Days, as bidden by your Lord, the Almighty, the All-Bountiful."

One of the most heinous of sexual offenses is the crime of rape. When a believer is a victim, she is entitled to the loving aid and support of the members of her community, and she is free to initiate action against the perpetrator under the law of the land should she wish to do so. If she becomes pregnant as a consequence of this assault, no pressure should be brought upon her by the Bahá'í institutions to marry. As to whether she should continue or terminate the pregnancy, it is for her to decide on the course of action she should follow, taking into consideration medical and other relevant factors, and in the light of the Bahá'í Teachings. If she gives birth to a child as a result of the rape, it is left to her discretion whether to seek financial support for the maintenance of the child from the father; however, his claim to any parental rights would, under Bahá'í law, be called into question, in view of the circumstances.

The Guardian has clarified, in letters written on his behalf, that "The Bahá'í Faith recognizes the value of the sex impulse," and that "The proper use of the sex instinct is the natural right of every individual, and it is precisely for this very purpose that the institution of marriage has been established." In this aspect of the marital relationship, as in all others, mutual consideration and respect should apply. If a Bahá'í woman suffers abuse or is subjected to rape by her husband, she has the right to turn to the Spiritual Assembly for assistance and counsel, or to seek legal protection. Such abuse would gravely jeopardize the continuation of the marriage, and could well lead to a condition of irreconcilable antipathy.

You have raised several questions about the treatment of children. It is clear from the Bahá'í Writings that a vital component of the education of children is the exercise of discipline. Shoghi Effendi has stated, in a letter written on his behalf about the education of children, that:

Discipline of some sort, whether physical, moral or intellectual is indeed indispensable, and no training can be said to be complete and fruitful if it disregards this element. The child when born is far from being perfect. It is not only helpless, but actually is imperfect, and even is naturally inclined towards evil. He should be trained, his natural inclinations harmonized, adjusted and controlled, and if necessary suppressed or regulated, so as to ensure his healthy physical and moral development. Bahá'í parents cannot simply adopt an attitude of nonresistance towards their children, particularly those who are unruly and violent by nature. It is not even sufficient that they should pray on their behalf. Rather they should endeavor to inculcate, gently and patiently, into their youthful minds such principles of moral conduct and initiate them into the principles and teachings of the Cause with such tactful and loving care as would enable them to become "true sons of God" and develop into loyal and intelligent citizens of His Kingdom. . . .

While the physical discipline of children is an acceptable part of their education and training, such actions are to be carried out "gently and patiently" and with "loving care," far removed from the anger and violence with which children are beaten and abused in some parts of the world. To treat children in such an abhorrent manner is a denial of their human rights, and a betrayal of the trust which the weak should have in the strong in a Bahá'í community.

It is difficult to imagine a more reprehensible perversion of human conduct than the sexual abuse of children, which finds its most debased form in incest. At a time in the fortunes of humanity when, in the words of the Guardian, "The perversion of human nature, the degradation of human conduct, the corruption and dissolution of human institutions, reveal themselves . . . in their worst and most revolting aspects," and when "the voice of human conscience is stilled," when "the sense of decency and shame is obscured," the Bahá'í institutions must be uncompromising and vigilant in their commitment to the protection of the children entrusted to their care, and must not allow either threats or appeals to expediency to divert them from their duty. A parent who is aware that the marriage partner is subjecting a child to such sexual abuse should not remain silent, but must take all necessary measures, with the assistance of the Spiritual Assembly or civil authorities if necessary, to bring about an immediate cessation of such grossly immoral behavior, and to promote healing and therapy.

Bahá'u'lláh has placed great emphasis on the duties of parents toward their children, and He has urged children to have gratitude in their hearts for their parents, whose good pleasure they should strive to win as a means of pleasing God Himself. However, He has indicated that under certain circumstances, the parents could be deprived of the right of parenthood as a consequence of their actions. The Universal House of Justice has the right to legislate on this matter. It has decided for the present that all cases should be referred to it in which the conduct or character of a parent appears to render him unworthy of having such parental rights as that of giving consent to marriage. Such questions could arise, for example, when a parent has committed incest, or when the child was conceived as a consequence of rape, and also when a parent consciously fails to protect the child from flagrant sexual abuse.

As humanity passes through the age of transition in its evolution to a world civilization which will be illuminated by spiritual values and will be distinguished by its justice and its unity, the role of the Bahá'í community is clear: it must accomplish a spiritual transformation of its members, and must offer to the world a model of the society destined to come into being through the power of the Revelation of Bahá'u'lláh. Membership in the Bahá'í community is open to all who accept Bahá'u'lláh as the Manifestation of God, and who thereupon embark on the process of changing their conduct and refining their character. It is inevitable that this community will, at times, be subject to delinquent behavior of members whose actions do not conform to the standards of the Teachings. At such times, the institutions of the Faith will not hesitate to apply Bahá'í law with justice and fairness in full confidence that this Divine Law is the means for the true happiness of all concerned.

However, it should be recognized that the ultimate solution to the problems of humanity lies not in penalties and punishments, but rather in spiritual education and illumination. 'Abdu'l-Bahá has written:

It is incumbent upon human society to expend all its forces on the education of the people, and to copiously water men's hearts with the sacred streams that pour down from the Realm of the All-Merciful, and to teach them the manners of Heaven and spiritual ways of life, until every member of the community of man will be schooled, refined, and exalted to such a degree of perfection that the very committing of a shameful act will seem in itself the direst infliction and most agonizing of punishments, and man will fly in terror and seek refuge in his God from the very idea of crime, as something far harsher and more grievous than the punishment assigned to it.

It is toward this goal that the community of the Greatest Name is striving, aided and reinforced by the limitless power of the Holy Spirit.

With loving Bahá'í greetings,
For Department of the Secretariat

Appendix 2:

Summary Policy Statement of the National Spiritual Assembly of the Bahá'ís of the United States on Domestic Violence

The statement that follows summarizes the policy of the National Spiritual Assembly of the Bahá'ís of the United States, the nine-member governing council of the Bahá'ís of the United States, toward domestic violence. The statement is published in a manual titled Guidelines for Spiritual Assemblies on Domestic Violence: A Supplement to Developing Distinctive Bahá'í Communities. *The manual was developed and published for the purpose of providing informed, consistent, and explicit guidance to Local Spiritual Assemblies* concerning domestic violence. Though the text of the manual is too long to include here, it is worth mentioning because it not only familiarizes Local Spiritual Assemblies with the many forms of domestic violence and eliminates misconceptions about it, but also brings together a selection of Bahá'í writings and authoritative guidance that provides solid insight into the roots of abuse in gender inequality, the effects of abuse on the spiritual development of individuals and society, the differing roles of education and punishment in its eradication, and means for addressing it in individual situations according to clearly enunciated spiritual principles.*

🐾 🐾 🐾

The National Spiritual Assembly wishes to convey a clear message that acts of domestic violence are at complete variance with the teachings of Bahá'u'lláh and that violence in the family is a practice to be condemned. In addition, domestic violence is a criminal act in the United States. Such behaviors, on the part of either men or women, are rooted in longstanding social practices connected with an inability or unwillingness to apply the fundamental spiritual principle of the equality of women and men and to recognize the

---

* A Local Spiritual Assembly is the annually elected nine-member governing council of a local Bahá'í community.

fundamental right of every human being to be treated with consideration and respect.

For the purposes of the work of the Bahá'í community, domestic violence should be understood broadly to include all forms of violence or abuse among family members or within the home. It encompasses behaviors in which one person uses coercion, intimidation, threats or violence to control the behavior of another. These behaviors usually escalate over time and may include verbal, physical, sexual, emotional, and economic abuses, as well as neglect, property damage, terrorizing, corrupting, and stalking. In addition to the spiritual consequences for one who commits such acts, the above behaviors are violations of Bahá'í standards of conduct and may result in loss of Bahá'í administrative rights. Many of these behaviors are also violations of state and federal law and may result in civil or criminal penalties.

In the Bahá'í administrative system, Local Spiritual Assemblies have primary responsibility for addressing situations of domestic violence. It is the National Spiritual Assembly's policy to actively support Local Assemblies in developing their capacity to recognize and effectively address domestic violence situations for the purpose of eradicating such deplorable behaviors from the life of the Bahá'í community. The National Spiritual Assembly's strategies include providing all Local Assemblies with detailed written guidance, as well as offering training and case-by-case assistance. Such written guidance and training materials are made widely available for use by Bahá'í communities and by Bahá'í institutions, schools, and organizations at all levels. As in other cases of violation of Bahá'í law, the sanction of removing an offender's Bahá'í administrative rights may be applied by the National Spiritual Assembly.

Recognizing that the functions of Local Assemblies and of various social service agencies and civil authorities are different and complementary, the National Spiritual Assembly encourages Local Assemblies to rely upon law enforcement and social service intervention in domestic violence situations, both for the immediate protection of individuals and for longer term needs. Local Assemblies are also responsible for assisting members of their communities to abide by Bahá'í standards of conduct, and they are encouraged to recommend to individuals the assistance of appropriate social services and counselors for this purpose. Therapeutic treatment is encouraged for both offenders and victims of domestic violence as a valuable component of healing and personal spiritual transformation.

In contrast to obvious and extreme forms of domestic violence the less extreme and non-criminal aspects of domestic violence present the challenge that they may not even be recognized as abusive. Yet they also are violations of Bahá'í standards of conduct, and they affect a broad segment of the population. Overcoming and preventing all forms of domestic violence requires that local Bahá'í communities foster a spirit and active pattern of loving support for families and emphasize both personal and family development in on-going education programs for children, youth, and adults. The National Spiritual Assembly promotes such education at the local and regional levels through sponsoring schools, developing curricula, and training teachers and facilitators. The Bahá'í community aims to create models of marriage and family life that are founded on respect, equality, justice, and unity and are conducive to the full human and spiritual development of every individual.

—The National Spiritual Assembly
of the Bahá'ís of the United States

Appendix 3:

Teaching Protective Behaviors to Young Children

When my grandson, Tanner, was three and a half years old, he asked his mother, "Who made all the people in the world?" My daughter-in-law, Kari, answered, "God made all the people, Tanner." Then he asked, "Did He make all the good people?" "Yes," she answered. "But who made all the bad people?" "Well, God made all the people, but He let them have choices and some people chose to do bad things. He didn't want them to do bad things, and it made Him sad when they did bad things," she replied.

The purpose of this appendix is to teach parents and children how to set boundaries with someone who might harm them, to prepare children ahead of time so they will know what to say or do. Knowledge of good boundaries helps children to avoid becoming a victim or a target of someone else's sickness, immorality, or perversion. It is written as though a parent is speaking to a child, giving the parent knowledge and language to use. I wish someone had written it for me when I was a child and that I had had it when my children were very young.

What Are Fences of Love?

Remember when you were very little and you had to stay protected inside the fence of your backyard? Well, a fence is like a boundary. You weren't allowed to go outside the fence so you would be protected from harm, because your parents loved you. This fence of love keeps out the people who might try to harm you.

God knew some people would choose to do harmful things, so he sent Prophets like Jesus, and Buddha, and Moses, and Bahá'u'lláh to teach us how to choose good behavior. He gave us rules like "love one another," and "be kind to one another," and, "Do unto others as you would have them do unto you." He also gave other rules like "Do not steal" and "Do not kill." Rules like this are called the laws of God. They are also called boundaries. And because God loves you, He doesn't want you to go beyond the limits or boundaries of His laws and commandments. They are like a fence of love that protects everyone in the world. This fence of love even protects the people who think about doing harmful things. God's laws inspire people to choose rightly.

What Kinds of Harmful Things Could People Do?

People could do hurting touch or secret touch. Hurting touch is hitting or slapping a child. Your mom and dad don't want anyone to do that to you. They want to protect you from someone who might do hurting touch.

Secret touch is touching you in your private places, and if someone does that to you, your mom and dad want you to tell someone about it right away.

Who Should You Tell?

Hold up your right hand and open up all your fingers so they are straight and tall. Your thumb is your mom. Tell her right away. If she's not around, your pointer finger is your dad. Tell him. Next to dad is your teacher. Tell your teacher right away, and she will call someone who will protect you. And the finger next to her or him is your grandma or your aunt. Your grandma and aunt love you very much and would not want someone to do hurting touch or secret touch to you. And your pinky finger is a policeman. You know he would protect you from harm. That's his job. You just keep on telling them that someone is doing secret touch, and don't stop telling until someone listens to you.

Your mom and dad even want you to keep telling if the person says they will do something bad to someone you love. And here's another part you must remember. It's important to tell someone even if it is mom, dad, grandma, grandpa, your aunt, uncle, brother, sister, cousin, or any other relative or friend of the family, who is doing secret touch.

Yucky Feelings

When someone does secret touch, you might have a yucky feeling inside. When you do, it's not because you have done something bad but because someone else did something God did not want him or her to do.

Private Places

It's important to know and remember that any place on your body where you can cross your arms and hands is private.[1] Nobody has the right to touch you in those places without your permission. If you cross your arms and hands over your private places, remember, no one has a right to touch you there.

Cross your arms and hands in front of your face now. No one has a right to touch you there without your permission. Now cross your hands and arms in front of your chest. No one has a right to touch you there. And cross your hands in front of your private place. No one has a right to touch you there. Now cross your hands behind your back where your bottom is. No one has the right to do secret touch there.

Remember that secret touch is the kind of touch that makes you feel yucky. You will feel better if you tell someone right away, because there's nothing so terrible that you can't say it out loud to someone that you trust and you know would never shame you.

Good touch, gentle touch, is something different. Good touch doesn't embarrass us or make us feel yucky. Good touch is like a friendly pat on the head or a nice handshake or a kind hug. But even this is only good with your permission. If you don't feel like hugging someone or don't want someone to touch you, all you have to do is say "no" very firmly.

Sometimes children get confused about what Bahá'u'lláh says. Remember how he tells us that he wants us to be kind? Well, children need to be protected from those who might do hurting touch or secret touch. We can say "no" to someone who is doing something wrong. Bahá'u'lláh gives us permission to say "no" out loud to protect ourselves from hurting touch and secret touch. That's setting boundaries with our power of speech. It's like putting a fence around our bodies so no one can get inside the fence and hurt us or make us feel yucky and uncomfortable.

Why Is It Important to
Learn about Boundaries?

It is important to learn about boundaries because you will have to tell people what your boundaries are when you are a teenager and when you become an adult. All throughout your life you will need to know how to protect yourself from harm. No one should ever do hurting touch to you, even when you are an adult.

We are taught by 'Abdu'l-Bahá* to pray to God for protection with prayers such as this one: "O God, guide me, protect me, make of me a shining lamp and a brilliant star. Thou art the Mighty and the Powerful."[2]

One of the ways God protects you is by providing you with parents who lovingly teach you about boundaries. We teach you to obey us because we don't want you to get hurt. When you learn how to obey your parents, you are learning how to obey God.

God wants us to protect ourselves with our power of speech. If you learn how to protect yourself with language and speech when you are a child, then when you are a teenager or an adult it will be easier to protect yourself. You will have knowledge, and that knowledge gives you power.

Talking with parents and teachers about problems like this gives us power to know what to do. When we talk together, it's called "consultation." With consultation about secret touch, the power to protect ourselves gets even stronger because we understand more. And when we understand more, we can help each other more. The most important thing that we understand is that the yucky feeling we have is because someone else did something that was wrong and

---

* The eldest son and appointed successor of Bahá'u'lláh.

that we want them to stop and never do it again. If anyone does secret touch or hurting touch to you and you feel yucky about it, then it is important to know that consultation or talking about it will help a lot.

Remember all those people on your right hand whom you can talk to? Your mom, dad, teacher, grandma, aunt, or a policeman? They are all there to help you, take care of you, and make sure no one harms you. They are there to put a fence of love around you to protect your boundaries around your body. So remember to talk to them and they will guide you.

Pray to God that He will protect you, too. And remember, nothing that can happen to you is so terrible that you can't say it out loud to someone that you trust and love and know would never hurt or shame you.

Guidance and Quotations for Parents

Please notice that the language I use in this discussion is "secret" touch and not "bad" touch. The reason for this choice is because it has been found that if children are told that someone has done "bad" touch to them, they will identify themselves as "bad" as well. That should be avoided at all costs.

The highest percentage of perpetrators of sexual abuse is actually family members, people whom children would not think of as bad, which makes the abuse even more confusing. All perpetrators of sexual abuse count on the fact that the children they seek to abuse have not been prepared by parents to know what to do if they are approached. A child who has not been prepared is an unguarded child. Teaching children protective behavior should be routine and should include having children memorize their address and tele-phone number and training them in social manners. Perpetrators also take advantage of the silence that surrounds the subject of sexual abuse. Our verbal guidance of children enables them to break the silence that has for centuries protected the perpetrators of such abuse.

As well-meaning parents, we may want to believe that others are as sincere as we are in obeying the commandments of God. Unfortu-nately, that is not the case, as Bahá'u'lláh advises, "Expect not that they who violate the ordinances of God will be trustworthy or sincere in the faith they profess. Avoid them, and preserve strict guard over thyself, lest their devices and mischief hurt thee. Turn away from them, and fix thy gaze upon God, thy Lord, the All-Glorious, the Most Bountiful. He that giveth up himself wholly to God, God shall, assuredly, be with him; and he that placeth his complete trust in God, God shall, verily, protect him from whatsoever may harm him, and shield him from the wickedness of every evil plotter."[3]

To safeguard the innocence and the good character of our chil-dren we must have knowledge of how to protect them from others who would do wrong to them out of ignorance, immorality, or pathology.

This information is a tool of perception, created for the purpose of teaching parents the necessity of setting firm boundaries, fences of love, for their children and teaching children how to set bound-aries for themselves. Knowledge of good boundaries helps us to maintain good character.

'Abdu'l-Bahá confirms the fact that education is the key: "The root cause of wrongdoing is ignorance, and we must therefore hold fast to the tools of perception and knowledge. Good character must be taught."[4]

It is important to treat others with compassion. However, there are some people who would take advantage of our compassion and kindness, thus creating a danger to the innocence and safety of our children. Therefore we must protect our children from them. The average person does not know the following statistic. The rate of recovery of those who perpetrate sexual abuse towards children is only 3 percent! Therefore we must be vigilant as well as compassionate. 'Abdu'l-Bahá warns us against those who practice deception: "Strive ye then with all your heart to treat compassionately all humankind—except for those who have some selfish, private motive, or some disease of the soul. Kindness cannot be shown the tyrant, the deceiver, or the thief, because, far from awakening them to the error of their ways, it maketh them to continue in their perversity as before."[5]

To deceive someone is to do something with a secret, private motive. This language is very much connected to the tyranny of sexual abuse—that is, secret touch, which is perverse behavior done in secret.

And though this concept is a far cry from Bahá'u'lláh's counsel to "Possess a pure, kindly and radiant heart," it is important to know that there really is no conflict with it.[6] As parents, we have a tremendous responsibility not to abdicate our duty to teach our children protective behavior. It is a kindness to them.

We cannot teach or encourage our children to hug everyone indiscriminately, because not all people are safe. Some are, but not all. We cannot teach intimacy and unity in our community without also teaching firm boundaries. And we cannot separate the need to teach our children principles of chastity from the importance of setting firm boundaries. In other words, we cannot "hammer" at our children about chastity without teaching them how to set boundaries with others. There are real dangers in the world, and it is just as important to transmit that concept to our children as it is to transmit the beautiful concept of all the virtues. Perhaps "caution" is also a virtue? And if it is a virtue, then we must readily give our children the knowledge of protective behavior so they can go fearlessly into the future. Teaching children protective behaviors should be as routine as teaching them to memorize their address, phone number, and other important information.

Appendix 4:

A Letter on the Spiritual Law of Chastity

May the following letter be understood in the context of reaching out to those who are seeking spiritual solutions to psychological problems. We cannot live in a moral-free world or with morally neutral belief systems and expect civilization to advance. There is too much at stake. Bahá'u'lláh's whole purpose as the Messenger of God for today is to bring about the unity and complete reorganization of the planet. I know many fine minds who see what is happening in the world yet are completely baffled by it. I believe that Bahá'u'lláh, as the divine physician, has his finger on the pulse of humanity and knows the remedy for the ills and issues that we face. I wrote the following letter in an effort to teach myself first and to address my own immorality.

Dearly loved Child of God,

It is with great respect for your openness and honesty regarding the topic of sex that I write this letter. I have spent the last few months studying literature on sex and intimacy as well as the Bahá'í writings in preparation for writing this letter. I hope not only to clear up confusion about appropriate use of the sex instinct, but I hope also to challenge you to meet your need for intimacy in ways that are spiritually fulfilling as well as growth enhancing.

From the moment of conception when our soul is created, it is clear that we are not meant to be alone. It is said that "man cannot live singly and alone. He is in need of continuous cooperation and mutual help."[1] We are meant to be connected and sheltered in intimacy and unity in the arms of our mothers and fathers during infancy. I suspect that we seek this primal intimacy forever in our relationships with others.

We humans are an interesting and sometimes confusing mixture of instincts, drives, impulses, and needs. Our instincts are the innate aspects of human behavior. They can be powerful impulses, yet can normally be adapted by obedience to the laws of God to order our lives and create a healthy society. Archeologist James Deetz says that culture is humanity's adaptive system. I believe that today the revelation of Bahá'u'lláh is the adaptive system by which our conditioned behavior is being changed, thereby changing our culture. Thus it is clear that our instincts do not govern our behavior. They are only impulses, and we do not have to act upon them. Behavior is chosen, and culture is shaped by our choices. Conversely, our choices can be shaped by the culture in which we live.

One of the instincts of a human being is sexuality. If one were to look only at the evidences in the media, literature, and the entertainment world, one would conclude that sexuality is all-powerful, uncontrollable, and the most important reason for living. It is not, of course. However, when teens are most vulnerable to biological stimulation, they view approximately fourteen thousand sexual images and references per year on television, not including the rest of the media.[2] This can skew their perception of what life, people, and sexuality are all about.

There are three components to human sexuality—biological, biopsychological, and personal. We have biological sexual organs for the purpose of mating. There is also an emotional component to our sexuality, which could be called bio-psychological. Through this we learn that certain aspects of people, objects, and situations can be sexually stimulating to our emotions. And there is a personal level through which the needs of our identity are fulfilled or satisfied by the intimacy that sexuality creates.

According to Capuchin priest Keith Clark, we have two basic needs as our identity develops. One is to be accepted by those who count. A second is the need to be ourselves.[3] I have come to believe that a third is the need to learn to subject our will to the will of God and to define our identity in relationship to God. The first two needs are fulfilled through intimacy. Though intimacy is closely connected to our sexuality, it is an even more fundamental need than sexuality. We crave intimacy, and true intimacy produces a calming of the soul.

Keith Clark and psychologist Erik Erikson define intimacy as the fusing of two or more people and the counterpointing of identities through self-awareness, self-disclosure, and the power of hearing. One person who has an awareness transmits that awareness to another individual through self-disclosure. That individual, after hearing the other, has an increased self-awareness, which he or she then discloses in counterpoint fashion (if they trust the individual), and intimacy is created.

What kind of self-disclosure creates self-awareness in another? Disclosing how you are distinguished from others—such as your parents, spouse, children, or friends—by attributes of your own helps to create such awareness. Disclosing what is important to you as a separate identity helps. Other types of disclosure that can help to produce self-awareness in others include disclosing your true self without hypocrisy or constraint and being accepted for who you are—not what you can do for the other—and disclosing who you are and where you fit in this world. Sharing your hopes, dreams, and goals; your sorrows; your beliefs; your knowledge; your questions about life in this world and the next, the spiritual truths you have discovered, the lessons of obedience you have learned—these, too, can be helpful. Disclosing what causes you pain, what makes you grateful, what makes you feel angry—all of this is self-disclosure that can lead the other person into a greater self-awareness as he or she examines his or her own identity and experiences. If we watch television for four hours per day, we will probably miss out on opportunities to achieve this deeper type of intimacy where soul meets soul.

If we seek intimacy only through romantic activity and what I call "genital behavior," we miss this greater intimacy. Entering into romantic activity with someone is a suggestion that you want to pursue the possibility of mating with that person. Participating in genital behavior is a promise that you are going to be there in the future for the sexual partner. This is the cultural meaning of these two types of behavior. If we act in ways that contradict or ignore the cultural meaning, we are, in effect, directly attacking and weakening society.

The Universal House of Justice, the international governing council of the Bahá'í Faith, writes in reference to the spiritual laws of God,

> Just as there are laws governing our physical lives, requiring that we must supply our bodies with certain foods, maintain them within a certain range of temperatures, and so forth, if we wish to avoid physical disabilities, so also there are laws governing our spiritual lives. These laws are revealed to mankind in each age by the Manifestation of God, and obedience to them is of vital importance if each human being, and mankind in general, is to develop properly and harmoniously. Moreover, these various aspects are interdependent. If an individual violates the spiritual laws for his own development, he will cause injury not only to himself but to the society in which he lives. Similarly, the condition of society has a direct effect on the individuals who must live within it.[4]

A letter written on behalf of Shoghi Effendi further explains,

> Briefly stated the Bahá'í conception of sex is based on the belief that chastity should be strictly practiced by both sexes, not

only because it is in itself highly commendable ethically, but also due to its being the only way to a happy and successful marital life. Sex relationships of any form, outside marriage, are not permissible therefore. . . .

The Bahá'í Faith recognizes the value of the sex impulse, but condemns its illegitimate and improper expression such as free love, companionate marriage and others, all of which it considers positively harmful to man and to the society in which he lives. The proper use of the sex instinct is the natural right of every individual, and it is precisely for this very purpose that the institution of marriage has been established. The Bahá'ís do not believe in the suppression of the sex impulse but in its regulation and control.[5]

Yet, how do we balance the need for chastity with our need for intimacy, and why can't some degree of romantic activity be allowed? Yes, intimacy is indeed created during romantic activity such as kissing and touching, but the end result for the two individuals involved, says a letter written on behalf of Shoghi Effendi,* is that it "often leads them to go too far, or arouses appetites which they cannot perhaps at the time satisfy legitimately through marriage, and the suppression of which is a strain on them." The letter explains that the spiritual law of chastity revealed by Bahá'u'lláh "certainly does not include the kissing that goes on in modern society."[6]

We can come to greater intimacy by holding hands and really getting to know the character of our potential friend or mate through the self-awareness, self-disclosure, and listening process that I mentioned earlier, far more completely than through romantic activity

---

* Shoghi Effendi Rabbání (1897–1957), the first and only Guardian of the Bahá'í Faith. He was the leader in succession to 'Abdu'l-Bahá from 1922 until his own death.

and genital behavior. In fact, holding hands with a very special person can be an electrifying experience. Savor it!

Just as parents wish babies came with a complete book of instructions, individuals sometimes wish they had a comprehensive list of dos and don'ts that would apply to every circumstance they might face. That might work in a world of automatons, but it won't work for people who are meant to develop their power of discernment through their own volition. A letter written on behalf of the Universal House of Justice to an individual states,

> "It is neither possible nor desirable for the Universal House of Justice to set forth a set of rules covering every situation. Rather it is the task of the individual believer to determine, according to his prayerful understanding of the [Bahá'í] Writings, precisely what his course of conduct should be in relationship to situations that he encounters in his daily life. If he is to fulfill his true mission in life as a follower of the Blessed Perfection,* he will pattern his life according to the Teachings. The believer cannot attain this objective merely by living according to a set of rigid regulations. When his life is oriented towards service to Bahá'u'lláh, and when every conscious act is performed within this frame of reference, he will not fail to achieve the true purpose of his life. . . ."[7]

Returning to the theme of intimacy: We also get to know another's character by observing them interact with others, by witnessing the congruence or incongruity of what they have revealed through self-disclosure and what they practice in reality, by meeting the mem-

---

* Bahá'u'lláh.

bers of their family and seeing how the family interacts, and by engaging in various activities together. These are the points that are necessary to confirming our choice of life-mate.

Contrast this stable way of choosing a life-mate with the following statement from Keith Clark: "Sexual activity which is no more than the gratification of urges and drives is frequently portrayed as fun and fulfilling. But conversations I have had over the years with those who engaged in sexual activity in such a way have convinced me that genital sexual activity and romantic behavior of themselves will eventually disappoint, not because they are bad, but because they are not enough. With insight we human beings can see that the species needs more human beings. That need for the species to continue gives meaning to human sexuality."[8]

Shoghi Effendi confirms the purpose of human sexuality, stating in a letter written on his behalf, "Bahá'u'lláh explicitly reveals in His Book of laws that the very purpose of marriage is the procreation of children who, when grown up, will be able to know God and to recognize and observe His Commandments and Laws as revealed through His Messengers.* Marriage is thus, according to the Bahá'í Teachings, primarily a social and moral act." 'Abdu'l-Bahá explains,

> Bahá'í marriage is the commitment of the two parties one to the other, and their mutual attachment of mind and heart. Each must, however, exercise the utmost care to become thoroughly acquainted with the character of the other, that the binding covenant between them may be a tie that will endure forever. Their purpose must be this: to become loving companions and comrades and at one with each other for time and eternity. . . .

---

* The Messengers of God, according to Bahá'í belief, include Moses, Abraham, Buddha, Krishna, Christ, Muḥammad, Bahá'u'lláh, and others.

The true marriage of Bahá'ís is this, that husband and wife should be united both physically and spiritually, that they may ever improve the spiritual life of each other, and may enjoy everlasting unity throughout all the worlds of God. This is Bahá'í marriage.[9]

I believe the true meaning and purpose of human sexuality must be understood within this context.

Because we are spiritual beings, our need for intimacy with other human beings also has a spiritual dimension, and this may be at the heart of Bahá'u'lláh's mission to unite the whole world. Keith Clark explains, "It [intimacy] is the deepest personal need we have, and it is a spiritual need. We long to come together with other human beings so that our spirits touch and our personalities fuse without being lost in each other. In intimacy the expanse which separates us from every other human being is bridged and the separateness, the insufficiency, the neediness which we inherit from our birth is temporarily alleviated."[10]

Clark also says that "human sexuality achieves its highest meaning when both the need for the species to be propagated and the need for intimacy are intended and pursued. Sexual activity which intends and pursues neither need ranks among humanity's most disappointing and devastating experiences. It has no meaning beyond the gratification of sexual urges and drives."[11] To avoid such mistakes we need to call ourselves to account on a daily basis and measure our behavior against Shoghi Effendi's definition of chastity:

> Such a chaste and holy life, with its implications of modesty, purity, temperance, decency, and clean-mindedness, involves no less than the exercise of moderation in all that pertains to dress, language, amusements, and all artistic and literary avocations. It demands daily vigilance in the control of one's carnal desires and

corrupt inclinations. It calls for the abandonment of a frivolous conduct, with its excessive attachment to trivial and often misdirected pleasures. It requires total abstinence from all alcoholic drinks, from opium, and from similar habit-forming drugs. It condemns the prostitution of art and of literature, the practices of nudism and of companionate marriage, infidelity in marital relationships, and all manner of promiscuity, of easy familiarity, and of sexual vices. It can tolerate no compromise with the theories, the standards, the habits, and the excesses of a decadent age. Nay rather it seeks to demonstrate, through the dynamic force of its example, the pernicious character of such theories, the falsity of such standards, the hollowness of such claims, the perversity of such habits, and the sacrilegious character of such excesses.[12]

In comparison to common social mores, such standards may at first sound extreme, but we are called by Bahá'u'lláh to "Cleave unto righteousness," to purify our characters, to correct our manners, and to improve our conduct because the sex instinct is not the all-powerful, uncontrollable force the media portrays it to be. We can gain spiritual insight from the truths that Bahá'u'lláh has revealed. His laws are "the highest means for the maintenance of order in the world" and the "keys" of God's "mercy" to His creatures.[13] Furthermore, our Creator has endowed us with the power of choice and an ever-developing power of discernment that can enable us to select the behavior that is in keeping with obedience to the will of God.

Since we crave intimacy and we know that it nurtures and calms the soul, it stands to reason that we need to become willing to commit to developing intimacy in community on a regular basis. We can do this through various means such as service to others, worship together, community development work, teaching others about God, and fellowship.

Besides craving intimacy, I believe that spiritually, because we were created noble, we hunger for chastity, too. Obedience to the law of chastity means that adults and young adults will make a full commitment to one another through marriage before children are born to them. Making a sacred commitment before God, family, and community strengthens the bond of marriage. If there is a firm commitment to one another, problems and differences that may occur in the future are more likely to be worked out.

Obedience to the spiritual law of chastity is not just an act of submission to God. It is a spiritual strength, a spiritual power. Every time we choose obedience, we strengthen ourselves spiritually. Furthermore, when we choose obedience, we are setting a beneficial example for others.

Obedience to the law of chastity implies that children should have faithfulness and obedience to the laws of God modeled for them by their parents. Children who have the benefit of such a role model in their parents will not be tormented with the conflict of values that plagues those of us who are caught between the inconsistent, seductive, irresponsible values of society and the challenging principles of moral conduct prescribed by the laws of God.

A letter written on behalf of Shoghi Effendi explains, "Chastity implies both before and after marriage an unsullied, chaste sex life. Before marriage absolutely chaste, after marriage absolutely faithful to one's chosen companion. Faithful in all sexual acts, faithful in word and in deed." The same letter further explains,

> The world today is submerged, amongst other things, in an over-exaggeration of the importance of physical love, and a dearth of spiritual values. In as far as possible the believers should try to realize this and rise above the level of their fellow-men who are, typical of all decadent periods in history, placing so much over-emphasis on the purely physical side of mating.

Outside of their normal legitimate married life they should seek to establish bonds of comradeship and love which are eternal and founded on the spiritual life of man, not on his physical life. This is one of the many fields in which it is incumbent on the Bahá'ís to set the example and lead the way to a true human standard of life, when the soul of man is exalted and his body but the tool for his enlightened spirit. Needless to say this does not preclude the living of a perfectly normal sex life in its legitimate channel of marriage.[15]

The spiritual law of chastity is there to strengthen us when we are weakened from observing those whom we admire, respect, honor, or cherish, break this law. We must remember in times of confusion that our chastity and obedience can help in the construction of a new and healthier world order.

Bahá'u'lláh tells us that our purity even has an effect upon the worlds of the spirit: "Purity and chastity . . . have been, and still are, the most great ornaments for the handmaidens of God.* God is My witness! The brightness of the light of chastity sheddeth its illumination upon the worlds of the spirit, and its fragrance is wafted even unto the Most Exalted Paradise."[16]

The law of chastity confirms that sex, though it is instinctive, is also learned behavior, as Ashley Montagu asserts in the following excerpt from an essay titled "The 'Sexual Instinct': A Good Example of the Role of Learning":

The so-called sexual instinct constitutes an outstanding example of the role of learning in what most people take to be a clear ex-

---

* Those who have declared their belief in Bahá'u'lláh are honored through their designation as "handmaidens" if they are female, and as "servants" if they are male. These titles signify recognition of their commitment to conform their behavior to Bahá'u'lláh's teachings.

ample of an instinctual drive. The truth is rather more interesting and revealing than that, for while all human beings, like other animals, are equipped with all the neurophysical arrangements and organs which have been evolved to function under particular conditions in certain ways we call sexual, they will, in fact, be able to respond only after a complex system of learning.

The "energies," as it were, fueling the sexual drive, which are largely hormonal, act upon a nervous system, which has to be taught how to direct and employ those "energies" and organs. In short, no one is born with the ability to perform sexually. Nor is this an ability which will develop with age in the absence of the appropriate conditioning stimuli. The capacity to perform sexually is one thing; the ability is quite another. The capacity is a potentiality which develops gradually and must be trained; that is learning must take place if the capacity is to become an ability. Difficult as it may be to believe, in the second half of the twentieth century, in an age of sexual freedom, in every civilized land for which information is available, there are to be found grown men and women of normal intelligence who enter upon marriage without the slightest idea of how to go about sexual intercourse or even, indeed, know that such a thing is possible. Almost every obstetrician, gynecologist, urologist, and marriage counselor of experience will have encountered such cases.

Unless the individual learns what to do with his or her sexual feelings or impulses, there is nothing in the body, brain or mind that will automatically lead the individual to sexual intercourse. The lack of any innate predeterminants for such behavior therefore conclusively eliminates it from the class of instincts.* This is

---

* Montagu is differentiating behavior from biological instincts here. It's an important distinction.

not to deny that all sorts of biological elements are involved in the development of sexual behavior, or that under normal conditions of social growth and development dispositions develop having as their object sexual behavior of some sort. But such sexual behavior requires the priming effect of learning if, for example, sexual intercourse is to be successfully accomplished. To call such dispositions "innate" is to obscure the fact that while many physiological changes are occurring in the developing individual the accompanying psychological changes frequently observed are largely influenced by cultural conditioning. Thus, for example, whether the object of sexual interest will ultimately be a member of the opposite sex or of one's own sex or of both sexes will, except in rare cases of prenatal hormonal sensitization, be culturally conditioned. Sex behavior changes observed in Western individuals, such as adolescent stress, gender identity, hypersexual activity, and the like, do not necessarily occur in individuals of other culture areas. Such changes, often attributed to "hormones" or other "innate" factors are, in any event, everywhere largely learned. Monkeys, apes, and humans, in that order, have become increasingly dependent upon learning in order to know what to do about their sexual impulses. Of course, hormones play a role in "fueling," as it were, the sexual impulses, but it is learning that determines the acquisition of the knowledge necessary for the practices of sexual relations.[17]

This information provides great consolation and relief to those who have been traumatized by sexual abuse in their childhood or adolescence and who may be acting out the abuse that was perpetrated upon them in their formative years. What others call "desire," we may truly call "pathology," and the call to chastity offers us great hope that we can overcome this learned behavior.

A question for those who have been traumatized by sexual abuse
is: Do we really want to act out a pathology that may lead us into
dark and dangerous ways, or do we make the choice of obedience,
trusting that our efforts toward chastity will not only heal us but in
some mysterious, and not a small way, promote the advancement
of civilization and world order?

A friend of mine who lives in Japan wrote to me concerning how
the repeated severing of sexual relationships wounds the soul. She
informed me that a few years ago, two Bahá'í doctors visited Japan
and gave a comprehensive talk to a group of university students on
the subject of chastity from a medical, psychological, social, and
spiritual point of view. The doctors' viewpoint was received very
well by the university students to whom they spoke. After talking
about the physical and social realities of the "new (or no) morality"
viewpoint, which include problems of pregnancy, disease, and ad-
dictive or arrested mental or emotional conditions, they talked about
the effect on the soul. They defined the soul as "anything that is
YOU that is NOT your body"—that is, your thoughts, feelings,
dreams, memories, and so on. Then they explained what things
affect the soul's health.

Sexual relationships involve both physical and spiritual connections. The doctors underscored this with notes about what happens
to the sympathetic and parasympathetic nervous system in sexual
relationships. A "bonding" that is later separated leaves a spiritual
wound—a "scar" on the soul, as it were. Many spiritual scars act
in the same way as physical scars do—the wounds may heal, but
they also leave one unable to feel as much as nature intended—at
least in spots. So some people, whether homosexual or heterosexual,
become "callous" if their behavior leads them into many broken
encounters. The ideal bond is one that is primary and eternal, not
confused, diluted, or disrupted.

The soul has great powers of recovery, the doctors emphasized, so it is never too late to return it to a better condition of health. But just as the body will decline in health and resilience if it is abused or neglected, one must be aware that the soul may lose some of its original sensitivity and elasticity if neglected or abused. It seemed to my friend that this explanation was very well received by the youth, who often wonder "why be chaste" and often get answers about physical or social dangers but few reasons that satisfy or protect the soul.[18]

When we are formulating our values, they need to be tested against a true standard. For those who recognize Bahá'u'lláh as the Messenger of God for this day and age, that touchstone is the revelation of Bahá'u'lláh. He has brought us the law of God to protect the individual soul as well as society. A letter written on behalf of Shoghi Effendi indicates "We must struggle against the evils in society by spiritual means, and by medical and social ones as well. We must be tolerant but uncompromising, understanding but immovable in our point of view."[19]

A commitment to chastity may require a commitment to celibacy. This means that one makes the choice to forego sexual or romantic pursuits, the true purpose of which is to prepare one for mating and genital involvement, which really is a promise to be there in the future for a sexual partner.

One finally finds the freedom he or she has been longing for when the commitment to chastity or celibacy is made once and for all. Swiss physician and psychiatrist Paul Tournier writes that such freedom is discovered "When a man feels in his heart that he is completely responsible for his behavior—that is when he may undergo a decisive moral experience which changes his life, frees him from the tyranny of his passions, and rebuilds his personality [identity]."[20]

There are fine nuances between our biological response and our romantic feelings, but one who is spiritually discerning can separate his or her biological response from the fact that this indeed is a moment of conscious choice to remain within the boundaries of the laws of God. Keith Clark tells us, "Sometimes a celibate is affected romantically and genitally by the relationships he or she has with others, but romance and genital activity are not pursued." He adds, "The unique demands of religious life do not dictate what a celibate feels and experiences but they do determine the behaviors we can choose and the kind of relationships we can form as a result of those behaviors."[21]

Science offers these amazing facts: Of the hundreds of chemicals that exist in the brain, some of them are there for the purposes of love and sexuality. These are associated with intense pleasure and can become powerfully addicting. Unregulated sexuality, then, can become like a powerful drug. Be aware that heavy-duty sexual fantasies can be symptomatic of unresolved sexual abuse, the memory of which may just be starting to surface.

No one knows who will become a drug addict after an initial experimentation with drugs. And no one knows who, in this oppressive, sexualized society will be lured into compulsive sexual activity.

If science tells us that some of the hundreds of chemicals in the brain exist for the purpose of love and sexuality and that we can become addicted to them, then it follows that, for the protection of society, they need to be regulated. God created us; therefore He knows us. His commandments have a scientific foundation. There is no "mystery" here, nothing arbitrary here. We know that sexually transmitted diseases are a leading cause of death in some groups. The rate of teen pregnancy is high. Women need to be protected from rape. The sexual slavery of women and children is rampant

---

* Literally "Most Holy Book," the primary repository of the laws and ordinances revealed by Bahá'u'lláh.

worldwide. The negative aspects of the media tease biology. God, through Bahá'u'lláh's revelation, is indicating that He wants these chemicals regulated within the institution of marriage for the protection of all members of society.

Bahá'u'lláh's revelation is bountifully available to all human beings at whatever stage of development they find themselves, regardless of whether they have declared a belief in him. His teachings and spiritual laws provide the nucleus of a new world order from which a purged and purified belief system will emerge in obedience to God. Bahá'u'lláh has exhorted us in his Kitáb-i-Aqdas* not to indulge our passions, and 'Abdu'l-Bahá encourages us to keep our "'secret thoughts pure.'"[22]

Bahá'u'lláh gently chides his followers, "Let your acts be a guide unto all mankind, for the professions of most men, be they high or low, differ from their conduct. It is through your deeds that ye can distinguish yourselves from others. Through them the brightness of your light can be shed upon the whole earth. Happy is the man that heedeth My counsel, and keepeth the precepts prescribed by Him Who is the All-Knowing, the All-Wise."[23]

A letter written on behalf of the Universal House of Justice tells us that when we courageously refuse to compromise the moral standards Bahá'u'lláh has set forth, we will be able to resist the corrosive forces that are so prevalent in society today:

There is no doubt that the standard of spotless chastity inculcated by Bahá'u'lláh in His teachings can be attained by the friends only when they stand forth firmly and courageously as uncompromising adherents of the Bahá'í way of life, fully conscious that they represent teachings which are the very antithesis of the corrosive forces which are so tragically destroying the fabric of man's moral values. The present trend in modern society and its conflict with our challenging principles of moral conduct, far from influencing the believers to compromise their resolve to adhere undeviatingly to the standards of purity and chastity set forth for them by their faith, must stimulate them to discharge their sacred obligations with determination and thus combat the evil forces undermining the foundations of individual morality.[24]

When confronted with the values of others that are in conflict with the moral standards Bahá'u'lláh has set, we are advised to fix our sight upon the supreme goal. Shoghi Effendi indicates that those who seek to live up to such standards

> should not look at the depraved condition of the society in which they live, nor at the evidences of moral degradation and frivolous conduct which the people around them display. They should not content themselves merely with relative distinction and excellence. Rather they should fix their gaze upon nobler heights by setting the counsels and exhortations of the Pen of Glory* as their supreme goal. Then it will be readily realized how numerous are the stages that still remain to be traversed and how far off the desired goal lies—a goal which is none other than exemplifying heavenly morals and virtues.[25]

If we pray for God to give us certitude regarding the law of chastity, we will put in motion the lessons that will enable us to acquire certitude and an expanded consciousness. We will have to accept the fact that others' belief systems may be different than ours and pray that God will help us to resolve the conflict of values and beliefs within our own mind; then our beliefs won't be tested every time we witness behavior that conflicts with the values we want to uphold.

---

* An allusion to Bahá'u'lláh.

I have come to believe that we are really helpless without the Word of God and without love for Bahá'u'lláh, which motivates us to follow his teachings and obey his law. He himself writes,

> Say: From My laws the sweet-smelling savor of My garment can be smelled, and by their aid the standards of victory will be planted upon the highest peaks. The Tongue of My power hath, from the heaven of My omnipotent glory, addressed to My creation these words: "Observe My commandments for the love of my beauty." Happy is the lover that hath inhaled the divine fragrance of his Best-Beloved from these words, laden with the perfume of a grace which no tongue can describe. By My life! He who hath drunk the choice wine of fairness from the hands of My bountiful favor, will circle around My commandments that shine above the Dayspring of My creation.
>
> Think not that We have revealed unto you a mere code of laws. Nay, rather, We have unsealed the choice Wine with the fingers of might and power. To this beareth witness that which the Pen of Revelation hath revealed. Meditate on this, O men of insight![26]

Do not doubt that steadfast obedience to the law of God has a powerful effect. The purpose of this physical life is, as the Universal House of Justice states,

> to prepare the soul for the next. Here one must learn to control and direct one's animal impulses, not to be a slave to them. Life in this world is a succession of tests and achievements, of falling short and of making new spiritual advances. Sometimes the course may seem very hard, but one can witness, again and again, that the soul who steadfastly obeys the law of Bahá'u'lláh, however hard it may seem, grows spiritually, while the one who compro-

mises with the law for the sake of his own apparent happiness is
seen to have been following a chimera; he does not attain the
happiness he sought, he retards his spiritual advance and often
brings new problems upon himself.[27]

The following prayer of 'Abdu'l-Bahá for firmness can help to
guide you to the steadfastness you desire. If you so desire, and if
you pray for strength, you will, indeed, become a banner of guidance to others as you live an exemplary life:

O my Lord and my Hope! Help Thou Thy loved ones to be
steadfast in Thy mighty Covenant, to remain faithful to Thy
manifest Cause, and to carry out the commandments Thou didst
set down for them in Thy Book of Splendors; that they may
become banners of guidance and lamps of the Company of above,
wellsprings of Thine infinite wisdom, and stars that lead aright,
as they shine down from the supernal sky. Verily, art Thou the
Invincible, the Almighty, the All-Powerful.[28]

My fervent prayers are with you that you might have certitude
concerning the law of chastity as it applies to these issues regarding
sexuality.

Warmly,
Phyllis K. Peterson

Notes

Introduction

1. Bahá'í International Community Office of Public Information, *The Prosperity of Humankind,* pp. 7, 8.

2. Bahá'u'lláh, *Tablets,* pp. 66–67.

3. Bahá'í International Community Office of Public Information, *The Prosperity of Humankind,* p. 10.

4. Bahá'u'lláh, *The Kitáb-i-Aqdas: The Most Holy Book,* ¶113.

Chapter 1: My Own Story

1. "authority." *Merriam-Webster Online Dictionary.* 2005. http://www.merriam-webster.com (21 June 2005).

2. "oppression." *Merriam-Webster Online Dictionary.* 2005. http://www.merriam-webster.com (21 June 2005).

3. Bahá'u'lláh, *Hidden Words,* Arabic, no. 2.

Chapter 2: Searching for Spiritual Identity

1. Bahá'u'lláh, *Seven Valleys,* p. 5.

2. Luke 12:34, 16:13.

3. 'Abdu'l-Bahá, *Some Answered Questions,* p. 38.

4. Bahá'u'lláh, *Seven Valleys,* p. 5.

5. Bahá'u'lláh, *Hidden Words,* Persian, no. 11.

6. Dhammapada 1 (J. Richards translation); attributed to 'Abdu'l-Bahá, in Helen S. Goodall and Ella Goodall Cooper, *Daily Lessons,* p. 85.

7 . 'Abdu'l-Bahá, *Paris Talks,* no. 18.2.

8. Bahá'u'lláh, *Gleanings,* p. 194.

9. 'Abdu'l-Bahá, *Paris Talks,* nos. 2.1, 17.10.

10. 'Abdu'l-Bahá, *Promulgation,* p. 291.

11. Ibid., p. 293.

12. Ibid., p. 31.

13. 'Abdu'l-Bahá, in *Auguste Forel and the Bahá'í Faith,* pp. 11–12.

14. 'Abdu'l-Bahá, *Promulgation*, p. 49.

15. Ibid., p. 172; Bahá'u'lláh, *Tablets*, p. 72.

16. 'Abdu'l-Bahá, in *Auguste Forel and the Bahá'í Faith*, p. 11.

17. 'Abdu'l-Bahá, *Promulgation*, p. 49.

18. Bahá'u'lláh, in *Bahá'í Prayers*, p. 308.

Chapter 3: Turning to the Light

1. Bahá'u'lláh, *Kitáb-i-Aqdas*, ¶123.

2. Bahá'u'lláh, in *Bahá'í Education*, p. 6.

3. Bahá'u'lláh, *Hidden Words*, Arabic, no. 31.

4. Bahá'u'lláh, *Kitáb-i-Íqán*, ¶278.

5. The Báb, in *Bahá'í Prayers*, p. 226.

Chapter 4: Telling the Secret

1. Bahá'u'lláh, *Gleanings*, p. 307.

2. Bahá'u'lláh, *Gleanings*, pp. 306–08.

3. Bahá'u'lláh, *The Seven Valleys and The Four Valleys*, p. 58.

4. Bahá'u'lláh, quoted in Shoghi Effendi, *Advent of Divine Justice*, p. 32.

5. 'Abdu'l-Bahá, *Secret of Divine Civilization*, p. 71.

6. Bahá'u'lláh, *Hidden Words*, Arabic, no. 40.

Chapter 5: Breaking the Intergenerational Cycle of Abuse

1. Bahá'u'lláh, *Kitáb-i-Aqdas*, ¶113.

2. Bahá'u'lláh, *Tablets*, pp. 34–35.

3. Universal House of Justice, *Messages*, no. 375.5.

Chapter 6: The Spiritual Aspects of Suffering

1. Bahá'u'lláh, *Gleanings,* p. 99.
2. Bahá'u'lláh, *Prayers and Meditations,* pp. 146–47.
3. Bahá'u'lláh, *Gleanings,* p. 106.

Chapter 7: Preventing and Treating Child Abuse

1. Bureau of Justice Statistics, "Sexual Assault of Young Children as Reported to Law Enforcement: Victim, Incident, and Offender Characteristics," US Department of Justice, http://www.ojp.usdoj.gov/bjs/abstract/saycrle.htm.
2. Ibid.
3. Ibid.
4. Letter on violence and sexual abuse of women and children, written on behalf of the Universal House of Justice, 24 January 1993, p. 1.
5. Ibid., p. 4.
6. Ibid.
7. Bahá'u'lláh, *Kitáb-i-Íqán,* ¶29, ¶30.

Appendix 3: Teaching Protective Behaviors to Young Children

1. In 1985 or 1986 I attended the Midwest Conference on Child Abuse, which is an annual event in Madison, Wisconsin. There one presenter offered in a workshop the idea of crossing the arms at various private areas of the body. Her name, alas, escapes me, but she affected my life, my thinking, and my teaching in a visual way. I owe her a big thank you and want her to know I will never forget her.
2. 'Abdu'l-Bahá, in *Bahá'í Prayers,* p. 29.
3. Bahá'u'lláh, *Gleanings,* p. 233.

4. 'Abdu'l-Bahá, *Selections from the Writings of 'Abdu'l-Bahá*, p. 136.

5. Ibid., p. 158.

6. Bahá'u'lláh, *Hidden Words*, Arabic, no. 1.

Appendix 4: A Letter on the Spiritual Law of Chastity

1. 'Abdu'l-Bahá, in *Foundations of World Unity*, p. 38.

2. See D. Kunkel, K. Cope, W. Farinola, E. Biely, E. Rollin, and E. Donnerstein, "Sex on TV: Content and Context," February 1999 (The Henry J. Kaiser Family Foundation).

3. Keith Clark, Capuchin, *Being Sexual . . . and Celibate*, p. 38.

4. Universal House of Justice, letter dated 6 February 1973 to all National Spiritual Assemblies, *Messages from the Universal House of Justice, 1963–1986*, no. 126.2.

5. Letter written on behalf of Shoghi Effendi, quoted in ibid., no. 126.7a.

6. Extract from a letter dated 19 October 1947 written on behalf of Shoghi Effendi to an individual, in *Lights of Guidance*, no. 1210.

7. Universal House of Justice, letter dated 17 October 1968 to an individual, *National Bahá'í Review*, No. 47, November 1971, p. 3.

8. Keith Clark, Capuchin, *Being Sexual . . . and Celibate*, pp. 27–28.

9. Extract from a letter dated 14 October 1935 written on behalf of Shoghi Effendi to an individual, in *Lights of Guidance*, no. 1160; 'Abdu'l-Bahá, from the *Selections from the Writings of 'Abdu'l-Bahá*, nos. 86.1–86.2.

10. Keith Clark, Capuchin, *Being Sexual . . . and Celibate*, p. 28.

11. Ibid., p. 29.

12. Shoghi Effendi, *Advent of Divine Justice*, p. 25.

13. Bahá'u'lláh, *Tablets*, p. 86; Bahá'u'lláh, *Kitáb-i-Aqdas*, ¶3, ¶2.

14. Extract from a letter dated 5 September 1938 written on behalf of Shoghi Effendi to an individual, in *Lights of Guidance*, no. 1157.

15. Extract from a letter dated 28 September 1941 written on behalf of Shoghi Effendi to an individual, in *Lights of Guidance*, no. 1211.

16. Bahá'u'lláh, quoted in Shoghi Effendi, *Advent of Divine Justice*, p. 32.

17. Ashley Montagu, *The Nature of Human Aggression*, pp. 72–73.

18. Dr. Marilyn Higgins, an authority on the moral development of children, personal correspondence with author, January 2001.

19. Extract from a letter dated 21 May 1954 written on behalf of Shoghi Effendi to an individual, in *Lights of Guidance*, no. 1221.

20. Paul Tournier, *The Person Reborn,* cover notes.

21. Keith Clark, Capuchin, *Being Sexual . . . and Celibate,* p. 108.

22. 'Abdu'l-Bahá, quoted in Universal House of Justice, extract from a letter to an individual, copy of which was sent to the compiler of *Lights of Guidance,* attached to a letter dated March 8, 1981.

23. Bahá'u'lláh, *Gleanings,* pp. 304–5.

24. Extract from a letter dated 22 May 1966 written on behalf of the Universal House of Justice to two individuals, in *Lights of Guidance,* no. 1219.

25. Shoghi Effendi, from a letter dated 30 October 1924 to the Spiritual Assembly of the Bahá'ís of Ṭihrán—Translated from the Persian, in *Lights of Guidance,* no. 457.

26. Bahá'u'lláh, *Kitáb-i-Aqdas,* ¶4.

27. Universal House of Justice, letter dated 6 February 1973 to all National Spiritual Assemblies, *Messages from the Universal House of Justice: 1963–1986,* no. 126.4.

28. 'Abdu'l-Bahá, *Bahá'í Prayers,* pp. 71–72.

Bibliography

Works of Bahá'u'lláh

Gleanings from the Writings of Bahá'u'lláh. 1st ps ed. Translated by Shoghi Effendi. Wilmette, IL: Bahá'í Publishing Trust, 1983.

The Hidden Words. Translated by Shoghi Effendi. Wilmette, IL: Bahá'í Publishing, 2002.

The Kitáb-i-Aqdas: The Most Holy Book. 1st ps ed. Wilmette, IL: Bahá'í Publishing Trust, 1993.

The Kitáb-i-Íqán: The Book of Certitude. Translated by Shoghi Effendi. Wilmette, IL: Bahá'í Publishing, 2003.

Prayers and Meditations. Translated by Shoghi Effendi. 1st ps ed. Wilmette, IL: Bahá'í Publishing Trust, 1987.

The Seven Valleys and the Four Valleys. Translated by Marzieh Gail and Ali-Kuli Khan. Wilmette, IL: Bahá'í Publishing Trust, 1991.

Tablets of Bahá'u'lláh revealed after the Kitáb-i-Aqdas. Compiled by the Research Department of the Universal House of Justice. Translated by Habib Taherzadeh et al. Wilmette, IL: Bahá'í Publishing Trust, 1988.

Works by 'Abdu'l-Bahá

Paris Talks: Addresses Given by 'Abdu'l-Bahá in Paris in 1911. 12th ed. London: Bahá'í Publishing Trust, 1995.

The Promulgation of Universal Peace: Talks Delivered by 'Abdu'l-Bahá during His Visit to the United States and Canada in 1912. Compiled by Howard MacNutt. 2d ed. Wilmette, IL: Bahá'í Publishing Trust, 1982.

The Secret of Divine Civilization. 1st pocket-size ed. Translated by Marzieh Gail and Ali-Kuli Khan. Wilmette, IL: Bahá'í Publishing Trust, 1990.

Some Answered Questions. Compiled and translated by Laura Clifford Barney. 1st pocket-size ed. Wilmette, IL: Bahá'í Publishing Trust, 1984.

Works of Shoghi Effendi

The Advent of Divine Justice. 1st pocket-size ed. Wilmette, IL: Bahá'í Publishing Trust, 1990.

Works of the Universal House of Justice

Messages from The Universal House of Justice, 1968–1973. Wilmette, IL: Bahá'í Publishing Trust, 1976.

Compilations

Bahá'u'lláh, 'Abdu'l-Bahá, and Shoghi Effendi. *Bahá'í Education: A Compilation.* Compiled by the Research Department of the Universal House of Justice. Wilmette, IL: Bahá'í Publishing Trust, 1977.

Bahá'u'lláh, the Báb, and 'Abdu'l-Bahá. *Bahá'í Prayers: A Selection of Prayers Revealed by Bahá'u'lláh, the Báb, and 'Abdu'l-Bahá.* New ed. Wilmette, IL: Bahá'í Publishing Trust, 1991.

Other Works

['Abdu'l-Bahá and Auguste Forel]. *Auguste Forel and the Bahá'í Faith.* Translated by Hélène Neri. Commentary by Peter Mühlschlegel. Oxford: George Ronald, 1978.

Ainscough, Carolyn, and Kay Toon. *Surviving Childhood Sexual Abuse: Practical Self-Help for Adults Who Were Sexually Abused as Children.* Rev. ed. N.p.: Fisher Books, 2000.

Bahá'í International Community—OPI. *The Prosperity of Humankind.* Wilmette, IL: Bahá'í Publishing Trust, 1995.

Bass, Ellen, and Laura Davis. *Beginning to Heal: A First Book for Survivors of Child Sexual Abuse.* New York, NY: Perennial, 1993.

———. *The Courage to Heal: A Guide for Women Survivors of Child Sexual Abuse.* New York, NY: Harper & Row, 1988.

Blume, E. Sue. *Secret Survivors.* New York, NY: Ballantine Books, 1991.

Bradshaw, John. *Bradshaw On: The Family.* 2d ed. Deerfield Beach, FL: Health Communications, 1996.

———. *Healing the Shame That Binds You.* Deerfield Beach, FL: Health Communications, 1988.

Bureau of Justice Statistics, "Sexual Assault of Young Children as Reported to Law Enforcement: Victim, Incident, and Offender Characteristics," US Department of Justice, http://www.ojp.usdoj.gov/bjs/abstract/saycrle.htm.

Crosson-Tower, Cynthia. *Understanding Child Abuse and Neglect.* Boston: Allyn & Bacon, Inc., 2004.

Danesh, H. B. *The Psychology of Spirituality: From Divided Self to Integrated Self.* 2nd ed. Wienacht, Switzerland: Landegg Academy Press, 1997.

Gil, Eliana. *Outgrowing the Pain: A Book for and about Adults Abused as Children.* San Francisco, CA: Launch Press, 1984.

Goodall, Helen S., and Ella Goodall Cooper. *Daily Lessons Received at 'Akká, January 1908.* Rev. ed. Wilmette, IL: Bahá'í Publishing Trust, 1979.

Hunter, Mic. *Abused Boys: The Neglected Victims of Sexual Abuse.* New York, NY: Ballantine, 1991.

Merriam-Webster Online Dictionary. 2005. http://www.merriam-webster.com (21 June 2005).

Miller, Alice. *For Your Own Good: Hidden Cruelty in Childrearing and the Roots of Violence.* New York, NY: Farrar, Straus, Giroux, 1984.

———. *Thou Shalt Not Be Aware: Society's Betrayal of the Child.* Preface by Lloyd DeMause. Translated by Hildegarde Hannum and Hunter Hannum. New York, NY: Farrar, Straus, and Giroux, 1998.

Miller, Mary Susan, Ph.D. *No Visible Wounds: Identifying Non-Physical Abuse of Women by Their Men.* New York, NY: Ballantine, 1996.

Penn, Michael, and Rahel Nardos. *Overcoming Violence against Women and Girls: The International Campaign to Eradicate a Worldwide Problem.* Lanham, MD: Rowman and Littlefield Publishers, 2003.

Richards, John., trans. *Dhammapada—Sayings of the Buddha.* See *Immerse, the Electronic Bahá'í Library* at http://havcamwiltrav.tripod.com/immerse/ or *Ocean Research Library,* a software library of the world's religious literature, at http://www.bahai-education.org/ocean/.

Romano McGraw, Patricia, Ph.D. *It's Not Your Fault: How Healing Relationships Change Your Brain & Can Help You Overcome a Painful Past.* Wilmette, IL: Bahá'í Publishing, 2004.

Sisk, Sheila L., and Charlotte Foster Hoffman. *Inside Scars: Incest Recovery as Told by a Survivor and Her Therapist.* Madison, AL: Pandora Press, 1987.

For more information about the Bahá'í Faith,
or to contact the Bahá'ís near you, visit
http://www.us.bahai.org/
or call
1-800-22-UNITE

PUBLISHING

Bahá'í Publishing and the Bahá'í Faith

Bahá'í Publishing produces books based on the teachings of the Bahá'í Faith. Founded nearly 160 years ago, the Bahá'í Faith has spread to some 235 nations and territories and is now accepted by more than five million people. The word "Bahá'í" means "follower of Bahá'u'lláh." Bahá'u'lláh, the founder of the Bahá'í Faith, asserted that he is the Messenger of God for all of humanity in this day. The cornerstone of his teachings is the establishment of the spiritual unity of humankind, which will be achieved by personal transformation and the application of clearly identified spiritual principles. Bahá'ís also believe that there is but one religion and that all the Messengers of God—among them Abraham, Zoroaster, Moses, Krishna, Buddha, Jesus, and Muḥammad—have progressively revealed its nature. Together, the world's great religions are expressions of a single, unfolding divine plan. Human beings, not God's Messengers, are the source of religious divisions, prejudices, and hatreds.

The Bahá'í Faith is not a sect or denomination of another religion, nor is it a cult or a social movement. Rather, it is a globally recognized independent world religion founded on new books of scripture revealed by Bahá'u'lláh.

Bahá'í Publishing is an imprint of the National Spiritual Assembly of the Bahá'ís of the United States.

Other Books Available from Bahá'í Publishing

The Challenge of Bahá'u'lláh

by Gary L. Matthews

Does God Still Speak to Humanity Today?

Members of the Bahá'í Faith, the youngest of the independent world religions, represent one of the most culturally, geographically, and economically diverse groups of people on the planet, yet all are firmly united in their belief that the prophet and founder of their faith—Bahá'u'lláh (1817–1892), a Persian nobleman by birth—is none other than the "Promised One" prophesied in the scriptures of the world's great religions. Bahá'u'lláh Himself claimed to be the Messenger of God for humanity in this day, the bearer of a new revelation from God that will transform the human race.

Author Gary Matthews addresses the central question that anyone investigating the life, character, and writings of Bahá'u'lláh must ask: Is this remarkable figure really Who He claims to be? The author explains why he believes the revelation of Bahá'u'lláh is not only divine in origin, but also represents a unique challenge of unequaled importance to humanity today. Matthews sets forth the claims of Bahá'u'lláh, summarizes His teachings, and then embarks on his own examination. His investigation correlates Bahá'í prophecies with developments in history and science; considers Bahá'u'lláh's knowledge, wisdom, and character; describes His ability to reveal scripture and what it was like to be in His presence; discusses the profound influence of His writings; and more. Matthews concludes by inviting readers to make their own analysis of the record.
$15.00 / $18.00 CAN
ISBN 1-931847-16-9

Close Connections:
The Bridge between Spiritual and Physical Reality

by John S. Hatcher

Is consciousness a product of the soul or an illusion the brain creates? Has creation always existed, or does it have a point of beginning? Is matter infinitely refinable, or is there some indivisible building block for all of physical creation?

Is the universe infinite or a finite "closed" system? Has the human being always been a distinct creation, or did we evolve from a lesser species? Is there a Creator whose design has guided the evolution of human society, or did creation and human society come about by pure chance? And if there is a Creator, why does He seem to allow injustice to thrive and the innocent to suffer so that we call natural disasters "acts of God"?

In Close Connections author and scholar John Hatcher employs axioms drawn from the Bahá'í Faith as tools for probing answers to these and other questions that relate to one overriding question: What is the purpose of physical reality? At the heart of the quest for these answers is a provocative analogy—a comparison of the creation and functioning of the individual human being with the method by which creation as a whole has come into being and progresses towards some as yet concealed destiny.

If the conclusions Hatcher draws from this study are correct, then every branch of science must in time reconsider its understanding of reality to include at least one additional dimension—the metaphysical or spiritual dimension—and its relationship to, and influence on, material reality.

$20.00 / $24.00 CAN
ISBN 1-931847-15-0

Prophet's Daughter: The Life and Legacy of Bahíyyih Khánum, Outstanding Heroine of the Bahá'í Faith

by Janet A. Khan

The remarkable story of a woman who shaped the course of religious history. Prophet's Daughter examines the extraordinary life of Bahíyyih Khánum (1846–1932), the daughter of Bahá'u'lláh, founder of the Bahá'í Faith. During the mid-nineteenth and early twentieth centuries, when women in the Middle East were largely invisible, deprived of education, and without status in their communities, Bahíyyih Khánum was an active participant in the religion's turbulent early years and contributed significantly both to the development of its administrative structure and to its emergence as a worldwide faith community. Her appointment to head the Bahá'í Faith during a critical period of transition stands unique in religious history.

Bahíyyih Khánum's response to the events in her life despite some eight decades of extreme hardship illustrates her ability to transcend the social and cultural constraints of the traditional Muslim society in which she lived. Optimistic and resilient in the face of relentless persecution and uncertainty, practical and resourceful by nature, she embraced change, took action, and looked to the future. The legacy of her life offers an inspiring model for thoughtful women and men who seek creative ways to deal with social change and the pressures of contemporary life.

$18.00 / $22.00 CAN
ISBN 1-931847-14-2

The Reality of Man

Compiled by Terry J. Cassiday, Christopher J. Martin, and Bahhaj Taherzadeh

What if it were possible for God to tell us why He created human beings? What if it were possible for Him to tell us the purpose of our existence?

Members of the Bahá'í Faith believe that just such information—and vastly more—is found in the revelation of Bahá'u'lláh, a body of work they consider to be the revealed word of God. Bahá'u'lláh, Whose given name was Mírzá Ḥusayn-'Alí (1817–1892), was a Persian nobleman Who claimed to receive a new revelation from God fulfilling prophetic expectations of all the major religions while laying the foundation for a world civilization.

The Reality of Man presents a glimpse of the unique depth, range, and creative potency of Bahá'u'lláh's writings on such fundamental questions as What is a human being? What is the purpose of human existence? Where did we come from? Is there a God? What is God like? Do we each have a preordained role or mission in life? Is there life after death? Are some religions "true" and others "false"? How can one evaluate religions? Prepared by the editors at Bahá'í Publishing, this compilation also includes writings from Bahá'u'lláh's eldest son and designated successor, 'Abdu'l-Bahá (1844–1921), whose written works Bahá'ís regard as authoritative.

ISBN 1-931847-17-7
$12.00 / $15.00 CAN

The Story of Bahá'u'lláh:
Promised One of All Religions

by Druzelle Cederquist

From the affluent courtyards of Tehran to the prison-city of Acre on the shores of the Mediterranean, The Story of Bahá'u'lláh brings to life in rich detail the compelling story of the prophet and founder of the Bahá'í Faith. Born to wealth and privilege, Bahá'u'lláh (1817–1892) was known as the "Father of the Poor" for His help to the needy. Yet despite His social standing, nothing could stop the forces that would have Him unjustly imprisoned in Tehran's notorious "Black Pit." Upon His release He was banished from Iran on a mountainous winter journey that His enemies hoped would kill Him.

Despite the schemes of His foes and the hardships of His exile, Bahá'u'lláh openly proclaimed the divine guidance revealed to Him. In over one hundred volumes, He delivered teachings on subjects ranging from the nobility of the soul to the prerequisites for the nations of the world to achieve a just and lasting peace.

The heart of His teaching was a new vision of the oneness of humanity and of the divine Messengers—among them Abraham, Moses, Buddha, Krishna, Christ, Muḥammad—Whom He claimed represent one "changeless Faith of God." Their teachings, He asserted, were the energizing force for the advancement of civilization. In 1863 Bahá'u'lláh announced He was the Messenger of God for humanity today and declared that His mission was to usher in the age of peace and prosperity prophesied in the scriptures of the world's great religions.

$15.00 / $18.00 CAN
ISBN 1-931847-13-4

To view our complete catalog, please visit

BahaiBooksUSA.com.